How to Take Action for Successful Performance Management

How to Take Action for Successful Performance Management

A Pragmatic Constructivist Approach

Falconer Mitchell
Hanne Nørreklit

BEP BUSINESS EXPERT PRESS

First published in 2019 by
Business Expert Press, LLC
222 East 46th Street, New York, NY 10017
www.businessexpertpress.com

ISBN-13: 978-1-63157-835-9 (paperback)
ISBN-13: 978-1-63157-836-6 (e-book)

Business Expert Press Managerial Accounting Collection

Collection ISSN: 2152-7113 (print)
Collection ISSN: 2152-7121 (electronic)

Cover image by boonchoke/shutterstock.com
Cover and interior design by S4Carlisle Publishing Services Private Ltd., Chennai, India

First edition: 2019

10 9 8 7 6 5 4 3 2 1

Printed in the United States of America.

Abstract

This book is intended for practitioners, students, and researchers who are interested in designing, using, assessing, and researching performance management systems. Managerial personnel involved in such activity will hold many beliefs about how their organization functions. This text uses the philosophy of pragmatic constructivism to show how managerial beliefs that underlie action can be made explicit and so facilitate their assessment and improvement. This involves recognizing and integrating the four dimensions (facts, possibilities, values, and communication) that represent how managers relate to the reality in which they operate. When managerial beliefs are based on an accurate representation of reality, they are more likely to be successful. Problems occur where reality is misrepresented in managerial beliefs. This is especially so in performance management, as the book illustrates using real-world examples. Specific topics addressed include planning and decision making, performance management of investment center managers, strategic performance management, and operational performance management.

Keywords

performance measurement, organizational actors, proactive truth, pragmatic truth, learning, dialogues, reflective actor

Contents

Preface

This book is intended for students and practitioners who work actively in developing, using, and assessing performance management systems for the construction of successfully functioning organizational practices. Organizational management personnel will hold many beliefs about how the organization for which they work functions. Such beliefs are constructed over time, tested out, revised, and fine-tuned on the basis of their experiences. Where beliefs are sound, intended action outcomes will be achieved, and when beliefs are unfounded, actions are likely to have unintended outcomes. Pragmatic construction is a philosophy that provides a basis for constructing and making explicit the beliefs that underlie management action. When a sound integration of four dimensions of reality—*facts, possibilities, values, and communication*—is achieved, then the consequent action is much more likely to result in the outcomes that management has intended. Based on the pragmatic constructivist conceptualization of human reality, this book develops concepts and methods that can be utilized for the effective performance management of organizational practices. It explains the core concepts of a pragmatic constructivist approach to performance management and provides specific applications of pragmatic constructivism for the core task of performance management action in a series of real-life case illustrations. More specifically, it addresses such topics as planning and decision making, performance management of investment center managers, strategic performance management, and operational performance management.

Acknowledgments

The authors gratefully acknowledge the constructive comments and input on the manuscript from Kenneth Merchant and the encouragement and patient support of Scott Isenberg.

CHAPTER 1

Introduction

Falconer Mitchell and Hanne Nørreklit

This book is concerned with the production and use of information for performance management. Performance management is considered to include the organizational planning and control processes that facilitate managers and employees in making decisions and help them take actions that are in the overall interest of the organization. For a performance management system to function effectively in planning and control, it has to be grounded in the business reality of an organization.

The pivotal point in the conventional wisdom of performance management is the objective measurement of the results of organizational activities and historical data–based estimations of consequences of decision alternatives. The relationships between action and observational points of measurement tend to be explained by a type of deterministic "natural law causality." However, such mechanical prescription for management practice might be damaging for organizational practices (Ghoshal 2005). For instance, there is a huge literature pointing to the flexibility inherent to the techniques used in performance measurement as well as the various short- and long-term dysfunctional effects of performance measurement on the actions of the managerial staff whose performance is assessed by their use (Merchant and Van der Stede 2012).

Overall, there are more dimensions involved in understanding human action than can be encompassed in the force of mechanical law, and there are no meta-empirical laws for running a business. The successes of companies such as LEGO and Apple did not happen because their top managers recognized and made employees adapt to some meta-laws for conducting business successfully. Rather, their successes are the result of organizational actors' efforts in developing and establishing a joint set of functioning activities, producing products and services that meet or even change peoples' values by introducing new functions and qualitative features in their lives. Hence, human actors are central to the construction of organized reality.

In view of that, this book considers pragmatic constructivism as a paradigm for understanding actors' construction of business practices to be performed. Pragmatic constructivism approaches organizational practices as constructed through the activities of the organizational "actors." Herein, the actors are organizational managers. Thus, an actor is a human being who participates in overseeing and conducting organizational activities with the intention of being a part of initiating and developing them. Driven by their own intentions and way of reasoning, actors create, influence, and control organizational activities in interaction with the organizational environment. From this perspective, they can be viewed as the coauthors of organizational activities. Organizational actors change, adapt, and align their actions and goals with existing organizational structures, routines, rules, and objectives. But since even the most specific instructions are to be interpreted and reflected within context of the situation in which specific practice occurs, managers and employees cannot function as adaptors only. They should also concerned about whether structures, routines, rules, and objectives are "reasonable." Accordingly, the practice of all actors, at all levels of the organization, is interactive, reflective, and innovative to some extent.

Actors do not act in a void but act in the physical, biological, human, and social world. Actors always act under presumptions of a specific perception and understanding of the world and creating a relationship with that world. They continuously construct, adjust, and reconstruct their relationship with the world in light of new experiences, contexts, and communication. The outcome of the actor–world relationship is a reality construction. The reality construction may be well-functioning and creating intentional results, or it may be ill-functioning and dominated by activities that do not succeed. The thesis of pragmatic constructivism is that the four dimensions of reality—*facts, possibilities, values, and communication*—must be integrated in the actor–world relationship if an actor's belief construct aims to form a successful basis for effective actions.

In the view of pragmatic constructivism, the shortcomings of the conventional approach to performance management do not imply that the management accounting tools for such purposes as planning and control are obsolete. Indeed, to observe and create a coordinated set of construct causalities across organizational activities, practitioners need to create a highly detailed and complex set of performance management models.

Based on the pragmatic constructivist conceptualization of human reality, this book discusses the concepts and methods developed for the performance management of organizational practices (Nørreklit 2017; Nørreklit et al. 2007, 2010). Part 1 of the book explains core concepts of a pragmatic constructivist approach to performance management while part 2 provides specific applications of pragmatic constructivism to the core task of performance management action in a series of real-life case illustrations. More specific, it addresses such topics as (i) core features of a successful construction of organizational reality, (ii) organizational actors and an actor-based method, (iii) planning and decision making, (iv) performance management of investment center managers, (v) strategic performance management, and (vi) operational performance management. It is intended for students and practitioners who work actively with developing, using, and assessing performance management systems.[1]

---

[1]See Jakobsen et al. (2019) for further details on how educators might use pragmatic constructivism as a paradigmatic base to prepare students of management accounting for the new demands of the role of trusted business partners in live practices.

PART I

Pragmatic Constructivism

CHAPTER 2

The Four Dimensions of Reality

Falconer Mitchell and Hanne Nørreklit

Introduction

This chapter provides an outline of how the four dimensions of pragmatic constructivism (facts, possibilities, values, and communication) relate to the actions involved in creating and using performance measures. It contains an explanation of each dimension in principal, as the nature of the dimensions for this type of action is situation specific and the detailed composition of each dimension is, therefore, particular to the prevailing circumstances extant within each organization when action is being determined. The latter chapters of the book complement this chapter by providing specific applications of pragmatic constructivism to performance measurement action in a series of case illustrations.

Performance measurement is viewed as a human action that can be predicated on a pragmatic constructivist framework (Nørreklit H. 2017; Nørreklit L. 2017; Nørreklit et al. 2007, 2010; 2013). However, performance measurement does not simply involve a single discrete action. Rather, it involves an interrelated series of actions comprising initiation (need for), design (planning), implementation (operation and use), and assessment (adjustment). All of these actions have to succeed if performance measurement is to be successful and pragmatic constructivism–based analysis can contribute to the success of all of these types of action.

Facts

The Nature of Facts

Facts can differ markedly in nature. First, there are facts that are a part of the physical work world. The existence and physical characteristics of land, machinery, vehicles, and buildings or of a workforce or a set of competitors would all possess this factual aspect. The physical aspects of a situation in which performance measurement action is to be taken can impinge directly on the type of measures that are needed. Performance is influenced by the physical resources available and so the success of a performance measurement system can be determined by its focus on the physical facts. A labor-intensive activity may require a very different approach to performance measurement than a capital-intensive one. Setting performance targets that are well beyond the capacity of physical resources is unlikely to be accepted for long by those subject to it.

Second, facts can be the creations (or constructs) of those involved. They can comprise beliefs and ideas about how things (including the physical) work in the work world. For example, the belief that quality issues originate from quality shortcomings of the employee as opposed to mechanical inadequacies of the production system has direct implications for performance measurement design. This type of fact is developed by individuals involved. It will reflect their observations, competencies, and experiences in the work world where they will continually appraise, absorb, and use the events that surround them. Many will reflect employee beliefs on why observed behavior is as it is found, that is, they relate to the factors that cause action. This type of fact can often be personal but may also be shared as a more general managerial belief in an organization. Although such beliefs exist and represent work world facts, they may have greater or lesser levels of accuracy. As time elapses they may be proved true or false. If they lack accuracy, then action based on them is likely to be unsuccessful. Consequently, people involved will seek out evidence that allows them to develop and substantiate their beliefs. This can be in the form of observed behavior that supports the belief, for example, a particular set of employees are motivated primarily by monetary rewards because their productivity rises when a bonus is paid to them. Thus, experience of the work world allows the assessment of this type of constructed fact.

The facts deemed relevant in a situation will, therefore, be the result of the learning that people experience in their work world over time. Beliefs will be hardened, modified, or jettisoned and new beliefs developed as evidence is gathered and assimilated.

The Role of Facts

The world in which people exist is constituted by facts. Consequently, it is the recognition of relevant facts in one's work world that will provide a foundation for successful action in initiatives such as designing and operationalizing performance measurement systems. Just as the successful detective can act to deduce the culprit of a crime from the evidence comprising the facts of the case, so the accountant or business person can recognize and use the pertinent facts as an initial basis toward the selection of the performance measures that will satisfy their needs for intelligence on organizational performance. Facts comprise the context or situation in which this type of action takes place. They, therefore, provide the grounding or foundation on which action can be based. If the wrong facts are selected or if the selected facts prove to be erroneous, then the efficacy of the performance measurement system will be compromised.

However, the organizational world is a dynamic one and it is likely that the fact-comprised situations pertaining to performance measurement in different organizations (and, indeed their parts) or within an organization at different points in time will be markedly divergent. The basis on which performance measurement action is built is, therefore, subject specific and susceptible to alteration rather than homogeneous and unchanging. This is why, general prescriptions on the specifics of performance measurement practice (e.g., the performance pyramid, the balanced scorecard, the performance prism) tend to be of dubious plausibility. The "law of each situation" must be paramount if action is to be successful. This creates the first of many challenges in performance measurement and is the subject of this chapter which explores the nature of facts in an organizational context, how they can be identified, and how they relate to performance measurement action. Exhibit 2.1 outlines how actions in performance measurement and facts are related.

Exhibit 2.1

Actions and facts

Actions	Facts
Initiate (need specification)	Objectives, Strengths, and Weaknesses
Design (set plans)	Problems, Constraints, and Capabilities
Implement (operate)	Resources
Assess (modify)	Constructs and beliefs

If each of the actions in the process of performance measurement is to be successful, then it has to be grounded in relevant facts. We have to know what we are trying to do (our factual objectives), we have to know what we have to do it with (our factual resources both physical and behavioral), we have to be aware of the challenges (the factual problems and constraints on action) and we have to possess credible ideas on how events occur in our work world (the factual constructs and beliefs about how things operate and function).

Possibilities

The Nature of Possibilities

The recognition of facts provides the base from which action possibilities can be identified. If these are reliably determined from the facts then they will be genuine possibilities with the potential that leads to successful action. Possible actions that do not adhere to the relevant facts are likely to be impossibilities and lead to unsuccessful action. The fact that I have $100 in my pocket provides an almost infinite list of spending action possibilities for me. Similarly, the organization with money assets will have great scope for spending action. However, normally action possibilities will not be as open ended as this simple money possession fact allows. A set of relevant facts will narrow the possibilities down considerably. The types of fact in Exhibit 2.1 on our needs, purposes, resourcing capabilities, and beliefs about variable relationships in the work situation will restrict the possibilities for action. Possibilities originate in the facts but must also fit (or integrate) with them if they are to be viable.

Identifying Possibilities

To illustrate the recognition of action possibilities in a performance measurement context, let us take the example of an organization that has a segment that is performing poorly (need), is a profit seeker (objective or purpose), has accounting expertise (resourcing), and has managers who believe that the causes of poor performance lie in the areas of staff expertise and the poor quality of output.

Initiation action will be founded in the factual beliefs of those involved as to the specification of the problem and the need for performance measures. Possible actions based on these facts will encompass such issues as (a) who to involve in designing the system, (b) how to communicate about it, (c) the extent and nature of consultation with those affected, and (d) the creation of a schedule of meetings to get the project underway. This will be followed by design actions. Here the possible performance measurement alternatives will be considered. For example, the use of a segment profit measure is likely to be considered given the organizational objectives and the need facts that exist. However, this decision gives rise to multiple accounting alternatives in respect to how profit is being measured. Should a profit contribution or a full profit be used? Should it be an operating, gross, or net profit? Should it be based on inventory valuation at full cost or variable cost? If significant inflation is a relevant and recognized fact, then should we use historic cost, current purchasing power, or replacement cost as the basis for profit measurement? Should the measures be linked to targets and rewards? The professional skill of the accountant will be needed to identify and explain the nature, meaning, and suitability of these types of measurement action possibilities. Furthermore, the possibilities of supplementing profit measurement will be considered. If product and staff quality have been identified as relevant facts, then these become aspects of performance that can merit specific attention. Nonfinancial measurements of these issues may become part of the performance measure package because of the factual belief of, at least some of those involved, that it is these factors that have caused profit deterioration. In these areas the expertise of production staff, engineers, and HR personnel can contribute to possible ways of measuring these factors. Their factual beliefs in the causality connections of profit-determining factors will ultimately be the source derivation of the performance measurement actions that are undertaken. This approach ensures that alternatives for action are identified and considered. This is a rational way of acting.

Once the most appropriate action possibility is selected (see subsequent section on values below) then actions required to implement the scheme have to be taken. At the design stage, the implementation possibilities will also have been identified in relation to the resource and belief facts identified and the preferred route to implementation selected. The same approach can be taken to implementation with alternatives vetted before action. Should implementation be trialed or simply started in full? Should the implementation be staged? Who will use the information generated? How will they use it? Finally, the measurement system, when in use, will generate evidence about the efficacy of the facts from which it has been derived. Are the beliefs about the causes of poor profitability defensible? Are actions taken improving performance? This new factual evidence will lead to further necessary modification action by permitting another round of consideration of the facts about system use and the possibilities it raises for changes to be made.

Values

The Nature of Values

Values are the motivators that allow people to choose between the action possibilities that confront them. At a personal level, values such as friendship, love, and philanthropy guide action. Similarly, professions have values of technical competence, ethics, and in the case of medicine the use of professional skills to assist others (i.e., the hippocratic oath) as determining action guidance. In organizations, values will also be present. These may be largely implicit and informal and simply reflect the ways of doing things that have been developed over time or they may be more explicit and contained informal statements of organizational creed or culture. Evidence of these values will be found in the organization's objectives and culture, which should directly reflect the values adopted.

Using Values

Many commercial organizations may have a shareholder value approach to business operations. The interests of the business owners will be paramount in deciding on the actions that they will take. A considerable literature exists on the implications of following this business philosophy (Rappaport 1997). When applied to performance measurement, it will ensure that the selected measurement systems report on how performance affects the wealth of and returns to the firm's shareholders. An "off the shelf" performance measurement structure that can support this approach is the balanced scorecard (Kaplan and Norton 1996). The strengths of this approach lie in the capitalist system's focus on ownership rights as the underlying engine of economic growth. This value drives economic activity and delivers wealth for many. Its weaknesses lie in the short-termism that it can promote (Merchant 1985; Merchant and Van der Stede 2012), which may lead to actions that compromise the longer-term health of the business. In this respect, performance measures may exacerbate the problem where they reinforce the short term orientation of many corporate managers.

In contrast, a broader set of values can be taken. This could encompass an ethical or a charitable focus and these values would promote performance measurement that would reflect these aspirations. Another way of broadening values would be to adopt stakeholder (as opposed to only shareholder) value. Here values would be considered not simply in respect of the shareholder group but also for employees, customers, suppliers, and government. The interests of all, or some of these parties, would then be incorporated in performance attainment and, consequently, in the measurement of it. The performance prism (Neely and Adams 2001; Neely 2007) would be an "off the shelf" structure aligned to this approach.

Values are therefore closely related to purpose, and it is purpose that directly motivates action. Not only does a clear knowledge of purpose allow action choices to be made, but it also facilitates assessment of actions taken. Their efficacy can be judged in relation to whether action has achieved what was intended by it (i.e., its purpose). Fitness for purpose can, therefore, provide a key test of whether organizational values are being attained.

Communication

The Nature of Communication

The fourth and last dimension of pragmatic constructivism is communication. An individual does not exist in isolation. People necessarily interact with each other before, during, and after actions are taken. Interaction with others requires effective communication among those involved. Human communication has multiple functions. For example, it facilitates knowledge gathering and dispersal, provides a means of consulting others and promoting participation, indicates and explains intention, demonstrates care and empathy, allows articulation of belief constructs, and gives a means of recording and appraising action. It may be largely based on language but it also involves mode of expression, demeanor, and action. Without good communication, relevant facts and possibilities may not be identified and values may be unrecognized, undeveloped, or not agreed upon. Thus, in the world of human interaction and cooperation, communication is an indispensable precursor to successful action.

The Role of Communication

In the process of action such as performance measurement, communication will play a role at each stage (see Exhibit 2.1).

First, communication is necessary to initiate and set objectives for new performance measures to be established. The recognition of the need for such change may initially be at the level of the individual. However, if this recognition is to be realized, others have also to be convinced of the need for it. Discussion involving the presentation of evidence (the case for new performance measurement) and persuasion of its merits are among the key oral and documented communication needed at this stage. In a nondictatorial organization, a consensus has to be built through communication to mobilize action.

Second, the nature of the new performance measurement has to be specified in the form of planned action. Here the discussion of possible measures and evaluation of their use will be needed. This is likely to be based on input from the range of staff involved in the proposed action. Topics here are numerous. Can the measurement data be readily accessed? How costly will this be? How reliable are the proposed measurements? Could they prove dysfunctional? Can they be matched to staff responsibilities? Also, to ensure ownership acceptance of the new measures, consultation with (and possibly the participation of) those subject to the new measures may be sought. All of these issues are central to the design stage and require extensive and effective communication between and among staff.

Third, the steps to put the new measurements into operation have to be taken. Putting the measures in place initially requires close monitoring and cooperation by all involved. This is a time for discussing the working of the new system and instituting the new reports and procedures such as the meetings needed to interpret and review and react to reported performance information. Given the nature of implementation, communication is central to the effective functioning of any new measurement system.

Fourth, once the new developments in performance measurement are up and running experience of them has to be evaluated. How well is purpose being attained? Does the original purpose remain appropriate? Are dysfunctional actions observable? Have reactions to information been apt? Issues related to assessment should be raised by those involved in designing, operating, using, and being subject to the new performance measures. Communication between and among these parties is an integral part of evaluating whether change has been successful.

Conclusions

The major role played by communication in all the stages of action means arrangements for its facilitation are strongly needed. The communication between staff members has to be ensured through meetings and contacts. Both lateral and horizontal communication mechanisms should be in place. Service staff, such as management accountants, need to interact with line functional staff as do supervisory staff and their subordinates. All can contribute ideas to improve action on performance measurement. However, they cannot do so without effective communication occurring at each stage of the performance measurement process.

CHAPTER 3

Integration of the Four Dimensions

Falconer Mitchell and Hanne Nørreklit

Introduction

Management will hold many beliefs about how the organization for which they work functions. These will be constructed over time and will be tested out, revised, and developed further on the basis of their experiences. The beliefs will be used in the process of management as a basis for designing, justifying, and gaining the support of others for policies undertaken. Thus, managerial action will be based on the beliefs that management hold. Where beliefs are sound, intended action outcomes will be achieved, and when beliefs are unfounded, actions are likely to have unintended outcomes.

Pragmatic construction provides a basis for constructing and making explicit the beliefs that underlie management action (Nørreklit H. 2017; Nørreklit L. 2017; Nørreklit et al. 2007, 2010). It does so by employing the four dimensions outlined in the previous chapter as a means of constructing sound beliefs. However, achieving this is dependent on the extent to which the dimensions are integrated, as it is through their integration that useful managerial beliefs are created and applied—see Exhibit 3.1. To provide the belief basis for successful management action, all the four dimensions must be in sync. They must fit together in a way that gives coherence to the beliefs that are constructed from them as the basis for management to act. When this coherence is achieved, the consequent action is much more likely to result in the outcomes that management has intended. The integration forms a basis for effective, functioning actions, or, in other words, it forms the basis of the establishment of "construct causalities" (Nørreklit H. 2017; Nørreklit L. 2017; Jakobsen et al. 2011).

Exhibit 3.1

Reality as integration of facts, possibilities, values, and communication

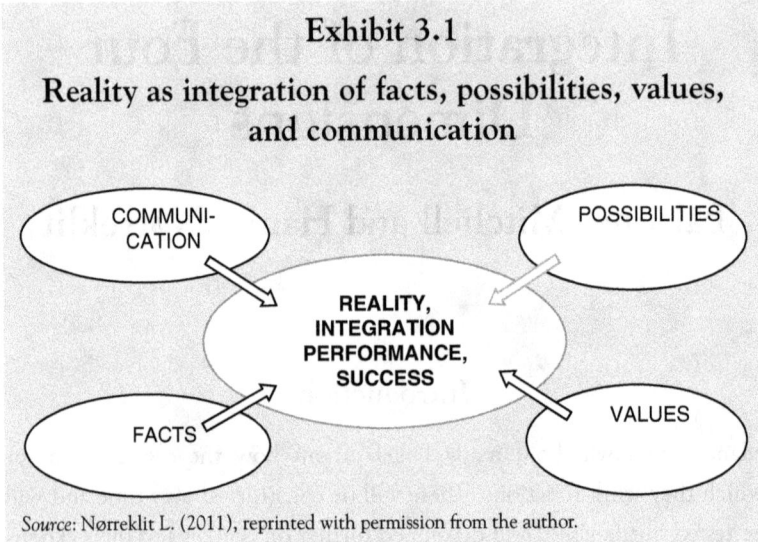

Source: Nørreklit L. (2011), reprinted with permission from the author.

Integrating the Dimensions

Facts selected as relevant from a situation confronting management provide the starting point. It is, of course, important that these facts are grounded in reality and are of significance to the issues management are considering as they provide the foundation for the integration of the said four dimensions. In performance measurement, it may well be the recognition of a problem that represents the factual base. For example, a need to improve the efficiency of manufacturing operations may be recognized as a fact supported by evidence of high costs and poor levels of profitability. This fact has to be refined and extended on the basis of the location and the magnitude of the issue being considered. Existing capabilities and resourcing needed to address the issue also have to be recognized as part of the factual specification.

Once the factual aspects defining the situation are in place, then the possibility dimension can be integrated with them. Possibilities are integrated with facts when they are derived from them. If they are not based on facts then they are likely to be based on fictions, and this will lead to

ill-informed actions. Also, the possibilities must match the facts identified, or there is the danger that they will become impossibilities. They
must be achievable from the capabilities and resourcing at the organization's disposal if they are to be viable. Moreover, the possibilities identified must address the factual situation that requires action to be taken.
Possibilities will vary in respect of their technical information content,
presentation, timing, interpretation, and use. However, they must all be
founded in the facts. If the issue relates to efficiency, then measurement of
this aspect must be made in a manner that will allow those involved to act
constructively to improve the situation. In this respect, the new performance measures should represent useful feedback that helps to identify why
efficiency is low as a precursor to taking appropriate corrective action;
that is, it fulfils a learning role. In addition, it may be that the possibility to ascertain whether efficiency is improving is also required, that is, a
feedback role. Thus, intentions for the new action are an important part
of specifying and indeed selecting possibilities for action. Possibilities also
have to be considered in respect of their potential for unintended outcomes. New efficiency measurements may create a focus on this aspect of
performance, which leads to a neglect of other important aspects of performance. For example, quality may become compromised or staff may
feel pressurized and react dysfunctionally to the new efficiency measures.
Possibilities for action should, therefore, take into account managerial
beliefs in all of their potential impacts. The reactions of those involved to
the creation of new performance information will be anticipated through
managerial beliefs about them. This is the great challenge of designing
performance measurement systems, that is, to get only what is sought or
intended by the action.

Values are the basis for choice among the possibilities for action that are
on offer. Thus, they also need to be considered when identifying the relevant
facts. If not, then any of the possibilities ascertained may preclude value
achievement. For example, if the job satisfaction of employee stakeholder
group is considered to be an important organizational value then their intrinsic motivations are likely to be an important situational fact that will
shape possibilities for action. In this way, possibilities are integrated with
both the fact and value dimensions and the selected action is more likely
to be coherent across these dimensions. Similarly, the organizational-level

values should be recognized and incorporated in fact-finding and possibility determination. Objectives involving profitability, stakeholder ambitions, ethics, fairness, and societal and environmental issues may all be components of the factual situation within which the organization operates. If they are not recognized as relevant facts then, again, action possibilities and selected actions may well preclude them. As a consequence, values will not be achieved by actions as the managerial beliefs determining action are not integrated with the true facts and possibilities. It is in the interaction between the dimensions that an integrative basis for sound action will be obtained.

As organizational management involves multiple individuals, communication is a key means by which the integration of the dimensions can be achieved. Managers have to collaborate to decide upon relevant facts and to determine the action possibilities that derive from them. They also have to agree upon what values are appropriate in any given situation and which facts and possibilities best relate to them. Communication will usually be a part of action as new developments have to be explained and understood. It is through communication that individual beliefs are exposed to scrutiny, discussion, and assessment. In this way, they can be refined and improved through the contributions of others.

Communication, thus, fulfils several functions that are necessary for actions to succeed. It allows for managerial beliefs to be exposed, assessed, and improved. Fact recognition, possibility identification, and value significance are all products of good integrated communication. The merging and spreading of the knowledge that can lead to successful action can only be achieved where communication is effective.

Integration and Managerial Beliefs

Pragmatic constructivism describes how people relate to the reality of their situations when deciding on taking action. This relationship is the basis upon which managers develop beliefs about how their organization operates. These beliefs are developed on fact relevance, possibilities for action inherent in the relevant facts, values to be attained, and appropriate communications (see Exhibit 3.2). One product of this analysis will be the construction of concepts as to how various factors relate together in complex causality connections, for example, what action possibilities will deliver intended outcomes. The accuracy of constructed managerial beliefs will, to a large extent, determine whether or not managerial actions can achieve their intentions successfully. Managerial beliefs are therefore crucial to action success. The integration of facts, possibilities, values, and communication will enhance the veracity of management's constructed beliefs as then they will be based on a sound conception of the reality of their situation. This section highlights four important issues that impinge on the integration of the four dimensions of pragmatic constructivism.

Exhibit 3.2

Core elements of pragmatic constructivism

THE MANAGER'S BELIEF

- Does the belief provide a successful basis for management action?
- Integration of facts, possibilities, values and communication forms a basis for successful action!
- Pre-action evaluation of beliefs – pro-active truth?
  - Are all four dimensions of reality integrated in the belief?
    - is it based on factual possibilities?
    - is it within the range of the organizational actors motivational values?
    - can it be communicated and understood by organizational actors across activities and institutions
- Post action outcome - pragmatic truth?
  - Does the belief leads to successful outcome?
- Learning process
  - Does the management minimise "truth gap" between pre action belief and post action outcome through an experience based reflective learning process.

Belief and Truth

If the constructed beliefs, upon which managers act, are true then it is more likely that managerial action based on them will be successful. However, the truth of a belief can only be unequivocally known after action has happened and the results of it are apparent. At the time of taking the action, outcomes are unknown and belief truth therefore remains unconfirmed. This creates a "truth gap" between belief pre- and post-action. A key skill of management is to minimize this gap through an experience-based learning process. Beliefs must be modified and refined as outcomes show where such improvement is needed. In this way, managerial intentions (underlying their actions) will be attained more fully over time.

Belief Multiplicity

Constructed managerial beliefs about complex causality connections in their business setting exist in profusion. They relate to technical, human, organizational, and financial matters. They range across functional specialties and will often contrast depending on the perspective from which they are taken. The accountant–versus–the engineer spectrum represents a strong example of divergent beliefs (Nørreklit 2011; Laine et al. 2016). Consequently, there is an ongoing need for beliefs to be exposed for enquiry and evaluation. This is how a multiplicity of beliefs can generate those possibilities which enjoy the strength of a consensus support and so are more readily operationalized.

Belief Coherence

Managerial beliefs have to be coherent if they are to be of value. At an individual level, internal capabilities must match external conditions. For example, our marketing and promotion efforts must take cognizance of the ability of our production units to deliver what is promised to customers. Performance measurement provides a key way of ensuring that such coherence is in place. Similarly, at an organizational level, for strategic objectives to be achieved, there has to be a coherent deployment of resources down the organizational hierarchy. Staff have to know what is expected of them to achieve set strategies. Again, performance intelligence will be critical to the achievement of this coherence. The business model, itself a construction of beliefs, must fit the strategy for which it is deployed.

Belief Change

The real organizational world is typically complex and dynamic. Beliefs about it cannot therefore be "cast in stone" as permanent truths. Observation of actions and interaction with others provides the evidence for modifying beliefs. If new performance measures do not have the intended results and have dysfunctional consequences, this must be assimilated and beliefs about them modified. Organizational life is a continuous learning process, and the beliefs and views of managers about it have to be amended and developed in response to managerial experiences. In other words, managers have to deal with their situation pragmatically.

Conclusions

Managers must ensure that they integrate the four dimensions of reality (facts, possibilities for action, values, and communication) that they experience. They must fit with each other if their beliefs about their organizational situation are to be sound and action based on them is to be successful. This provides a solid foundation for the many actions required of management.

CHAPTER 4

The Actors and the Actor-Based Method

Falconer Mitchell and Hanne Nørreklit

Introduction

Pragmatic constructivism implies that the production and use of performance measures for the construction of functioning practice require a reflective actor interacting with the practice context. Conceptual models are vehicles for the actor's reflection and analysis, and methodology is the linking tool between theory and practice. If performance management concepts are to be useful to practice, then they must be articulated together with a methodology apparatus that practitioners can use in their construction of functioning activities.

Standard textbooks (Anthony and Govindarajan 2007; Kaplan and Atkinson 2015) within the area of performance management propose a set of practical performance measurement tools that will aid decision making and performance evaluation in an organization through formalized and systematic processes. But these texts neither take into account the individuals' perceptions and thinking of factual possibilities nor their emotions, intuition, and values (Vaivio 2008). Mainly employees are perceived as a component in a system that has the role of serving the interests of the whole system, that is, the company. In the following, we conceptualize the actors and a method to include them in performance management activities.

The Actors' Way of Reasoning

Human beings are complex, creative, reflective, and adaptive. However, they are driven by fairly consistent intentional values and ways of reasoning that they apply when constructing their relationship with the world. Thus, one force influencing the individual actor's or group of actors' action in creating reality constructions is their intentional values (von Wright 1983; Nørreklit et al. 2007, 2010). The individual actor's or group of actors' intentional values can be scrutinized through the wishes and wants they express for themselves and others when planning and evaluating actions and reality constructions.

Another force influencing the individual's action is their way of reasoning (Nørreklit et al. 2007; Cetina 2001; Trenca and Nørreklit 2017), which shapes the relationship between the actor's intentionality and the actor's interaction with the world. It is related to the actor's perception and understanding of the reality construction he or she has created and the course of actions that the person considers are required to initiate a change from an existing situation to another situation that the person intends to happen. The changes are constructed through a set of more or less implicit principles and methods according to which one set of values and possibility-loaded facts leads to another set of values and possibility-loaded facts through the experience of a set of specific courses of action. Actors construct the system of applied methods through analysis and reflection on their situation where existing methods can enter as vehicles for the actor's reflection and analysis (Nørreklit et al. 2016). In order to function according to intention, the actor's way of reasoning about action methods should facilitate the creation of construct causality through the integration of facts, possibilities, values, and communication. Coordinating with other actors' intentional values and reasoning is a particular aspect of an actor's way of reasoning.

Exhibit 4.1 provides examples of actors' different values and ways of reasoning within a fast-growing company. The examples illustrate that the organizational managers are motivated by different intentional values and that they apply different ways of reasoning for the course of actions that they consider are required in the company to create a successful outcome. The president's values and way of reasoning are dominated by growth and optimism with only little concern for profit and consolidation. The sales manager's values and way of reasoning are characterized by an aggressive marketing policy, where pricing is made according to short-term profit considerations; that is, only variable costs are taken into consideration. The accountant is influenced by order and stability, where pricing is based on a full-cost calculation.

Exhibit 4.1

Examples of a firm's different actors' way of reasoning

President and owner [MA in fine arts and sculpture]: I want the company to be big. I want to make a big and fast turnover. I use the philosophy "Buy low, sell high, collect the money early and pay later." I make the customers pay in advance. This way we finance our growth. One can use accountants for administrating figures, taxes, etc. We need them for cash flow budgets and cost calculations. One has to know the product costs. But otherwise, accountants are so depressing to talk to. They always think the worst will happen. The sales manager and I have a lot of fun together. He is optimistic and has ideas, but he's "tough"—he has no feelings.

Manager of sales and marketing [MA in sales and marketing]: I will not say no to an order because of the price. A full-cost theory is ridiculous. We will take an order if it covers more than variable costs. Competition is tough, and it is important to be in front. I have raised my salesmen to adapt solutions to the customers' needs. Our engineering department is not good enough at adapting to the customers' needs. They make too many mistakes and lack control. The organization must be more efficient in order to keep up with the sales department.

Manager of production [MA in engineering]: The customers run the firm, and the sales department thinks too shortsightedly. We have too many urgent orders required by the sales department. And it is impossible to use the sales forecast because it is too unreliable; so I make my own sales forecast. The situation in the engineering department is chaotic for the reason that they cannot stand the pressure from the sales department. I think the firm must appoint a chief engineer who will prioritize orders and projects and improve planning.

Manager of engineering [MA in technical engineering]: The sales department tells us what they want, and then we try to do it. If the sales department changes priorities, which happens often, then we follow sales in changing our priorities too. The sales department gets angry if we do not supply what they want. I like to follow the new technological

(continued)

development, but I do not like to manage. So I would like the firm to get a new manager for the engineering department.

Head accountant [MA in accounting]: We must cover all our costs when we price a product. I would like to be able to stop the operations of the company for some weeks just to organize and coordinate the activities properly. We have problems all over the company. I use most of my time putting water on the fire.

Performance management in a firm is about coordinating management decisions and actions in an economically sustainable way. If the organizational managers are not economically minded, then the management accountant must try to influence their values and way of reasoning through performance management. It demands that the managers accept and understand the values and reasoning embedded in the performance management system. The understanding must be reciprocal, however. Not only must the managers understand the performance management system, but the system must also understand the managers, and, hence, the management accountant must understand the managers' values and ways of reasoning in respect to doing business and the often highly specialized functional activities. To make all of the functional areas of the firm work together in the construction of functioning activities, it is necessary to have a method for creating and developing the organizational actors' mutual understanding of each other's values and way of reasoning. The actor-based method can be used as the tool.

The Actor-Based Method

Consistent with pragmatic constructivism, the actor-based method assumes that people alternate between interacting and reflecting (Arbnor and Bjerke 2008). The actor-based method consists of four phases—(1) preunderstanding, (2) understanding, (3) diagnosis, and (4) postunderstanding—that the actor should follow during a research process or when constructing knowledge in more general terms, for instance, as management accountants in an organization. The actor-based method is open for a number of methodological procedures. For instance, in order to solve *matter-of-fact questions* (Arbnor and Bjerke 2008) various quantitative and qualitative methods may be applied. However, an individual's grasping the human practice behind the numbers and conceptualizing their own life condition is evident within the actor-based method. In the following, we describe the method from the perspective of a management accountant considering the construction of a performance management system. Also in the chapters to follow, the actor-based method will continue underline discussions.

Preunderstanding

In the preunderstanding phase, the management accountant gathers factual information about the situation in the company, objectives, structures, people, challenges and strengths, and performance management problems through the view of the initiating manager. This should enable an understanding of the manager's view of the company's goals and strategies and motivations and goals for performance management. From this background, managers and management accountants make a preliminary determination of the performance management problem to be solved and the results to be achieved. The task is preliminary because what in the beginning seems to be one kind of problem may turn out to be a totally different one after more information is collected and analyzed. This is different from a method based on objectivity (a perspective frequently adopted by accountants). Also, at this stage, it enables a preunderstanding of the conceptual models that might be relevant for solving the tasks.

Understanding

In the process of understanding, the management accountant gets to know each relevant employee's intentional values, professional skills and tasks, relationship and cooperation with other functions and employees, perception of the performance management problem, and thoughts about the system to be used to solve the problem. This is ascertained through a series of dialogues. Dialogue, rather than a questionnaire, is used to reveal this because it can avoid precategorized patterns of thinking. Dialogue is a dynamic and reflective process of conversation between two or more persons. In the dialogue, information flows on several levels and concepts of reality get reflected and are developed.

Throughout the overall process of understanding, management accountants review these dialogues and other material and summarize their understanding and interpretation of the actors' intentional values and model governing their thinking and action. They search for important and meaningful concepts and structures in the demands and requirements they have for the performance management system. The employees' demands and hopes for the system form the basis of their idea of a performance management system, which is then presented to the employees. Employees and the management accountant discuss and comment on the system idea using dialogue, through which the employees' knowledge and understanding of the system idea develops. Furthermore, their engagement with and the possibility for developing and using the system are evaluated. Managers are continuously presented with various types of information on development in the project, including that of system idea, problems, possibilities, and development, in the formulation of management control and accounting tasks.

Diagnosis

In the diagnosis phase, problems are identified. Reviewing the collected documents and the related dialogue, management accountants search for an understanding of the performance measurement task and, if necessary, continue to work theoretically in pursuit of an appropriate system. They form an overview of the task of constructing the system by identifying system possibilities using their factual ascertainment of the work situation and evaluating resource demands and employees' understanding and acceptance of the system. Furthermore, the application of the system idea together with its ability to solve management control tasks and problems is evaluated. This leads to an evaluation of the system development task that is required to overcome problems and gaps. The diagnoses are discussed with the managers, and the system development procedures are tested and evaluated by the employees involved. Here, communication using appropriate language to influence and agree or disagree with actors' thinking patterns plays a critical role.

Postunderstanding

In the postunderstanding phase, the system is developed and implemented. Simultaneously, feedback from participating employees is collected and the system is tested to see if it is working. The results of the method depend on the management accountant's technical skills and ability to minimize the gap between the expected results and the pragmatic results through an experience-based learning process.

Conclusions

Drawing on pragmatic constructivism, we argue that methodology is the linking tool between performance measurement models and organizational practice. If performance management concepts are to be useful to practice, they must articulate together with an actor-based method that practitioners can use in their construction and use of performance measurement systems.

Overall, the actor-based approach involves interactive and reflective processes that help achieve a higher diagnostic certainty about the performance management system's abilities to facilitate construct causality. An integrated part of the pragmatic constructivist way of applying the actor-based method lies in the interplay between proactive truth and pragmatic truth. This forms the basis of the learning process that aims to diminish the truth gap; that is, it is expected that the ex-ante pragmatic constructivist–based diagnoses will become more accurate with experience. The focus on the integration of the four dimensions of the reality construction is at the core of a pragmatic constructivist way of applying the actor-based method. Thereby, it differs from a radical social constructivist approach, which focuses mainly on the dimension of communication.

Discussion Questions

1. Following conventional thinking on performance management, what are the main methodological steps to follow in the design and implementation of performance measurement systems? What are the perceptions of management and employees in this model you have proposed? What are the strengths and weaknesses of conventional approach?

2. Drawing on the actor-based approach, you are asked to design and implement a performance measurement system for an organization. How would you proceed? What are the challenges of the approach?

PART II

Application of Performance Measurement Action

CHAPTER 5

Interactive and Reflective Planning and Decision Making

Falconer Mitchell, Hanne Nørreklit, and Lars Braad Nielsen

Insights from This Case Study

Based on the ideas of pragmatic constructivism, this chapter outlines a conceptual framework showing how organizations (represented by coalitions of decision makers) can structure their planning and decision-making activities (and incorporate financial information to support them) in complex and uncertain contexts. A reflective managerial approach is outlined. This involves multipronged communication and cooperation to integrate the four dimensions of pragmatic constructivism: facts, action possibilities, values, and communications. The conceptual framework is illustrated by a case study.

Conceptual Framework

Complexities of Management

Traditionally, educational accounting literature on planning and decision making assumes that accounting information is provided for individual use (Bhimani et al. 2008; Kaplan and Atkinson 2015). This literature also takes for granted that reliable intelligence on alternative courses of action for these purposes is readily available. In reality, managerial ability to specify future alternative options and to predict their financial and organizational impact is constrained due to the complexity and dynamism of the business world. Inevitably, planning and decision making will frequently involve highly subjective estimation by managers. Managerial views on the practicality and beneficial attributes of action possibilities will underpin forecasting activity. Managers have recourse to the facts that define their situation and will attempt to identify the complex causality connections (construct causality) that exist among the facts on which they have information. Knowledge of these relationships can help strengthen the forecasts that they develop about the future possibilities for action that confront them. Where the context in which management operates is highly complex and changeable these causality linkages are much more involved but less obvious. This is often the case where strategic concerns involving external factors exist, as information frequently becomes increasingly uncertain. In these situations, managers' lack of comprehension about the financial implications of the options that confront them and about the nature of the prevailing causality connections means their actions are lacking in certainty. Moreover, the intrinsic values of one manager may differ from another and from those of their firm. This may motivate the manager to manipulate the uncertain information at their disposal in order to achieve their own ends (March 1987).

Further planning and decision-making complications are caused by the fact that these activities mostly involve groups of managers (as opposed to individual managers). In situations where each manager in a decision group holds different beliefs about the facts and their implications and also have different values conflicts can arise and compromises and deals can occur that weaken decision-making rationality that accounting texts assume exists.

As a result of unrealistic assumptions in textbooks about managerial planning and decision making, it is necessary to consider how these activities take place in the real world where information is uncertain, managers lack rationality, and group interactions permeate the role of management (Nielsen et al. 2015, Norreklit et al. 2017). The following section outlines a structure for planning and decision making in a realistic context that reflects the above complexities. Ideas from pragmatic constructivism are used to achieve this aim.

A More Realistic Managerial Model

Pragmatic constructivism implies that information accuracy is an important part of managerial planning and decision making. At the point of making a plan or a decision the future is unknown. It cannot, therefore, be claimed that information used is completely true. The information used has to be estimated, and these estimates are termed proactive truth. The accuracy of proactive truth can only be verified when events have actually happened and real outcomes are known. This actual information is termed the *pragmatic truth*. Since decisions are based on proactive truth, it is imperative to assess the extent to which pragmatic truth confirms these estimates. If there is a divergence between these two truths, it will reflect the uncertainty under which management operates (Norreklit et al. 2007, Mitchell et al. 2013).

Uncertainty in planning and decision making is created by the difficulty in recognizing complex causality connections in prominent situational factors and by the inability to recognize properly the four dimensions of pragmatic constructivism (relevant facts, the possibilities they create, values, and needed communications). Both sets of issues are related, and improving the knowledge about the four dimensions and their integration can provide insights about the complex causality connections that exist.

Identifying the future impact of managerial action, therefore, requires a deeper analysis of the four dimensions of pragmatic constructivism. A thoughtful, ongoing review of initial beliefs against actual outcomes facilitates understanding of how beliefs need to be altered. This process can be termed the *learning theory of truth*. When this becomes well-developed, a sound comprehension of the relevance of situational factors to decisions is created, and this in turn helps in identifying why events did not unfold as was initially expected. All of this reviewing and analysis develop managerial experience that enhances future planning and decision making. Creating sound assumptions about decision impacts (causality connections) improves when managers can identify the relevant facts that constitute the reality of their situation and the action possibilities inherent in them. The fit of these possibilities to facts and values and the use of appropriate communications provide an analytical integration that facilitates recognition of causality connections.

However, forecasts and actuals are unlikely not to show any variance and the gaps that emerge between proactive and pragmatic truths should be an important focus for management. Analysis of the causes of this gap is a key basis for improving management awareness and understanding of the causality connections that can enhance future estimates and reduce the truth gap.

Strategic and Operational Action

The decisions taken by managers can be broadly split into two categories: strategic and operational. Both are related to managerial assessments of the complex causality connections that define the situation in which they function. Business strategy involves the development and use of an overall business approach designed to succeed in a given environment in which the firm operates. Thus, many of the complex causality connections pertinent to strategy relate to the interactions between the firm and its environment. The strategies established provide the managerial group with a focus that enables them to take decisions in a cohesive, consistent, and coherent manner. They must act in concert to ensure overall effectiveness of the strategies to be implemented.

Planning and decision making at this level is designed to bring together all of the functional areas of the firm as a working whole. The business model defined at the strategic level will need the support of a financial model that can generate information on the financial impact of different strategic decisions. These models will also provide the structure within which planning and decision making will take place at the operational level.

Operational planning and decision making also require the involvement of different types of functional managers. Here too, financial information on action possibilities is needed. This financial information has to reflect the complex causality connections that are created through the interactions between the managerial groups involved. This financial information is, therefore, a manifestation of identified causality connections and represents key feedback to management that helps them to both identify and reduce the truth gaps that they experience.

In the following case, the role of management accounting in planning and decision making at an operational level is described (in Chapter 7, strategic issues are considered). The case also highlights the challenges of identifying the complex causality connections pertinent to operational planning and decision making. It shows how these considerations are dealt with during new product development from the initial-ideas phase through full-scale production. The integration of accounting information in this process is also reviewed.

The Case of HEALTH

HEALTH is a large Scandinavian firm. It employs over 7,000 people and operates in over 60 countries. Its organizational structure comprises three main functional areas: R&D, production, and retail. Their longstanding corporate ethos has been to improve the quality of life for those using their therapeutic products. They expect to generate profits that are sustainable and so business can proceed in a stable manner. These medical and financial values are the substance of their corporate culture (see also Exhibit 7.2). The following case shows how complex causality connections (construct causality) relating to the development of new products are developed and how management accounting plays a key role in this aspect of their planning and decision making.

Developing Construct Causality Connections in the Flow of New Products

New Product Development Scheme

HEALTH's planning and decision making are based around a new product conduit. This represents a framework covering the development of new products from initial proposals to full-scale manufacture and sale. New product proposals surface as tentative suggestions to create new worth based on the key skills of the firm in accord with their established strategy. Suitability for market is an essential feature to be verified, as early as possible, by marketing managers.

The proposals are developed into an expected product characteristics plan—see Exhibit 5.1. This describes what the new product is expected to achieve both functionally and financially. It passes through several review points designed to increase knowledge about how the product's potential can be realized. Each review point covers staffing, logistics, work processes, and technology needs. In effect, these reviews strengthen the comprehension of the relevant complex causality connections that underlie the achievement of proposals.

From both customer and supplier perspectives, the nature of a new product remains highly indeterminate at the start of the flow conduit.

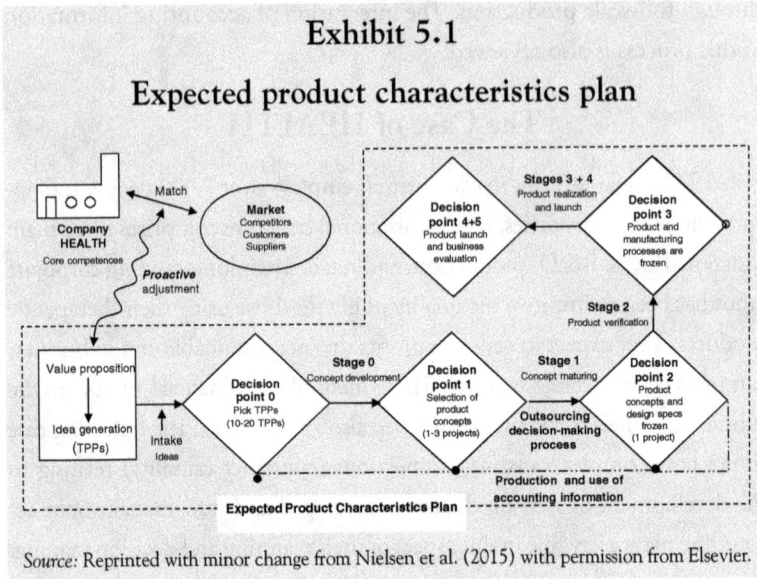

Exhibit 5.1

Expected product characteristics plan

Source: Reprinted with minor change from Nielsen et al. (2015) with permission from Elsevier.

As the proposal progresses, in-house skills and knowledge provides a basis for generating planned practical actions to deliver the product. This enables possibilities to be restricted, and at decision point 1 only three conceptual possibilities are allowed for consideration. Decision point 2 restricts the product plan to one concept, and design characteristics and production logistics are firmed up in both technical and financial terms. Production process plans are also finalized. At decision point 3, the detailed plans start to become reality with equipment put in place, material supply arranged, and staffing scheduled. Commitment begins at this point with the chosen possibility finalized. Following this, the new product is launched and a start made on comparing actual results to expectations to determine and review causes of any truth gaps found.

This overall process, therefore, facilitates recognition of relevant facts, selects the most viable possibility that matches firm values, and fosters the communication necessary to create the product. Together, these constitute the complex causality connections that define the creation of new products.

Ongoing Integrative Efforts

Development of a new product thus involves ongoing reviews where new action possibilities that fit core values are proposed and nonviable proposals dropped. The reviews are carried out by multifunctional groups of experienced staff. Achieving the plans set for the product is a major objective of these reviews. These review groups are, in effect, judging whether proactive truths have become pragmatic truths.

Financial information about the new product is produced at each decision point. It reflects key aspects of the underlying causality connections, and in the event the financial results intended are not being met, the product may be dropped or moved back in the flow conduit for modification.

Ensuring the provision of credible financial information about new products is challenging especially in the early stages of product development. There is a progressive hardening of this information as the new product develops with its design becoming clearer and production characteristics becoming more and more factual. The comparison of financial plans with actual outcomes provides the review group with attention-directing information that is a source of learning and improvement for the review group staff.

Multifunctional Contribution

The conduit flow framework allows many staff to contribute to the success of the new product. This is the reason for using multifunctional review groups. These groups facilitate lateral communication based on different areas of expertise so that reviews and actions are well-informed as to what is possible and what meets the firm's needs and values. Contributions come from production, sales, procurement, finance, and R&D. This fosters integration and helps to both ensure new products emerge as technically and financially attainable and the firm's values and the needs of potential customers are met. In the following section, the use of accounting information throughout the flow conduit is discussed in more detail.

Use of Accounting Information by Review Groups

In the flow conduit, each review group will use accounting information at each decision point. Initially, figures are approximate and comprise only tentative sales revenues and R&D costs. These are accompanied by descriptions of how new products fit in with set strategies. As the new product progresses through its developmental phase, subsequent decision points involve the creation of more detailed product cost and sales figures with estimates of the possibility and timing of product launch in the market. These data are presented formally in spreadsheet models for each new product proposal. These also outline the product's financial characteristics (e.g., breakeven, operational gearing) and the best other possibilities with which it can be compared. The spreadsheet model encompasses sales revenues, direct costs, gross profits, cash flows, and the net present values (NPVs). These estimates are agreed upon by the review groups who then assume ownership of them.

Cooperation during the Early Life of the New Product

The early part of the product's life involves development of prototypes and selection of production equipment to be used. The prototypes provide evidence to create the case for the product, particularly for its sales value and production cost. A target contribution margin, set at a strategic level, has to be attained.

To estimate sales revenue, marketing managers consult regional staff to estimate sales volumes for the new product proposal:

> From the start, we make a volume forecast for the development project. It will be revised as we go through the project. The volume forecast is driven by marketing with input from the subsidiaries. They talk to the sales companies and ask what do they think about this product and so on?

However, to enhance the objectivity or realism of sales estimates, statisticians and modelers question them repeatedly. The estimates are screened against those of similar products:

> In the business analytics department, we have some dedicated statistics and market-modeling professionals who evaluate the forecasts. They say: "You have considered that England can have an uptake of the product like this. If we look at launches, then we can see that usually we have an uptake that looks like this. So, do you think it's realistic? Why is it that this product can sell more?" And then it is that they have to go in and defend why exactly this product has so much better uptake than the last three we have

launched in the same area. And if they cannot defend it, then we say: "well, then we do not invest in it."

Thus, the analysis includes historic factual information as well as new estimates. Comparison and review of the figures result in a best estimate as judged by the review group. This estimate is considered to be in concert with the factual evidence available to the group. The proactive truth is thus strengthened as much as possible before it can be assessed in the light of actual results (i.e., pragmatic truth). To further strengthen the accuracy of estimates, some staff bonuses are awarded based on how accurate the sales estimates turned out to be. This is done to reduce staff motivation to manipulate results:

> We measure marketing on the accuracy of their estimates, especially what is at decision point 3, where we decide to go out and make investments.

Cost information on new products is focused on direct costs and is produced by accountants in consultation with engineers. The engineers supply information on equipment capacities, staffing requirements for equipment operation, and resources needed for logistics. Accountants then produce product costs for both small-scale pilot production and full-scale production later at overseas locations.

> We are good at estimating cost price. It is not so difficult to estimate what we call variable costs. It's a question of setting up material lists and estimating some material unit prices and some waste rates—and how much wages should be put into it. And then it depends on where it should be produced. Sometimes, we know that we start production in Denmark—but to make it transparent in relation to the market and to increase the incentive to sell the product, we give them a fixed cost price. We use the cost price we expect to reach when the product is produced where it should be for the rest of its lifetime. So, most often, it may be that we start in Denmark, then our global operations takes a loss on this, which we then gain later. But we have to, because if we bring the real cost price to our subsidiaries, then it is not interesting for them to sell the new product. Also, such targets that are set from the beginning increase our incentive to keep the cost price down.

In addition, accountants provide information support to production staff who carry out assessments of parts of the manufacturing process that may be contracted out. This is supplemented by the procurement team that gathers quotes from different suppliers for components. All of these efforts support the achievement of cost targets while ensuring the firm retains its core competencies.

Thus, there are four overlapping analyses in the firm's new product development. First, engineering and production predominate in the creation of the prototype and the specification of the required equipment. Second, procurement dominates in the sourcing of product supplies. Third, sales dominates in ensuring that the product fits customer needs. Fourth, accounting dominates in product cost calculations. In this way, different specialist knowledge is brought to new product development. Engineering and procurement ensure a factual technical foundation, sales assures that customer needs are considered, and accountants emphasize the need for product profitability. Together, these interacting analyses enhance the realism and construct causality of the new product plans as all of these specialist managers work together to address the new product complexity and uncertainty that the firm faces.

Final-Approval Decision-Point Management

At decision point 3, equipment is purchased, suppliers are established, and production begins. Costs, therefore, become known at this stage although sales figures won't be available as yet. Sales estimates retain some uncertainty. To ensure supply arrangements are not overprovided, HEALTH delays some investment decisions at this point. Commitment to all possibilities in respect of manufacture is restricted:

> We are cautious about how much money we invest in manufacturing to achieve the volume. We look at what we have, how flexible we can be, and how late we can go in and then decide to spend the money. And that is what we can do. After all, it is where we can be reasonable. That is, we delay investments as much as possible but at the same time say that if it actually goes as they have forecasted then we can follow it. Because this is the opposite problem. So, we must not be so careful that if they actually sell the volumes that marketing has said, then we cannot deliver it.

Thus, despite the predecision point 3 preparatory work, HEALTH remains tentative in its commitments. This approach is fostered by part manual production and outsourcing of some components that reduces investment commitments. To harden sales estimates, product examples are tested on customers. The firm tries to have as high a factual backing as possible for sales estimates before all investment takes place. Production arrangements are kept as flexible as possible, and although unit costs remain high as a consequence because large-scale production is delayed, investment risk is reduced.

Decision Points 4 and 5 and the Revelation of Pragmatic Truth

Finally, full product launch occurs at decision point 4. Updates of financial information estimates begin to arrive as product characteristics and supplier terms become factual. After decision point 4, the actual product sales are closely monitored using a system the firm has installed in hospitals worldwide. In case of unfavorable deviations in costs, an improvement process is undertaken to keep costs down:

> We are often too optimistic about how fast we can reach the target cost price. There is a learning curve effect especially when we speak of new product platforms. But in general, we are optimistic. And this produces some projects after product launch, where we must lower the cost price. So there's something to do there.

Decision point 5 is the finish of the new product conduit flow. It generates feedback for future new product planning and decision making. Sales achievements are verified against estimates as are costs against profits. Thus, at this point, the differences between proactive truth and pragmatic truth become apparent, that is, the truth gap. HEALTH has been rather successful in reducing the truth gaps in relation to product costs and the sales volume of mature products. However, it faces challenges in estimating the sales volume of new products:

> Where we make the most mistakes is on the users' readiness to try a new product. When we come up with new improved products, we continue to have the confidence that if we sell it well and explain well what it is, then they will also try it. They just don't. It takes a very long time.

Conclusions

This case describes managerial activity that is in accord with the concepts of pragmatic constructivism. Health's analytical process is designed to identify and use the complex causality connections that underpin their processes of new product development. This knowledge facilitates the generation of action possibilities and financial consequences as part of an ongoing managerial review and learning process. All key managerial specialists are brought together to contribute their expertise, and their interaction helps create sound new products and related accounting estimates that are incorporated in their decision making. Valuable managerial experience is built up as products pass through the flow conduit. As this happens the factual nature of the product and the estimates harden and action possibilities become more determinate. Firm values are maintained through incentivization and reinforced through communication.

Thus, the case study demonstrates that many of the characteristics of pragmatic constructivism can be successfully employed in dynamic and complex business situations. The four dimensions are paramount in the pursuit of factual information, its use to select and define an action course that meets established values, and the facilitation of the communication channels needed to achieve these activities successfully.

Discussion Questions

1. How does conventional thinking on planning and decision making compare to the four dimensions of pragmatic constructivism?

2. From a perspective of pragmatic constructivism, organize a planning and decision-making process (in outline) for an organization of your choice. How will you arrange the planning and decision processes? How will accounting information be produced? How can information quality be validated?

CHAPTER 6

Performance Management of Investment Center Managers

Falconer Mitchell and Hanne Nørreklit

Insights from This Case Study

The governance of decentralized corporations involves the HQ-management transfer of their decision-making authority to investment center managers. Conventional thinking of principal–agent theory looks at the investment center managers as opportunistic agents who should be motivated and monitored through performance contracts. However, performance measures are reductive and can have serious dysfunctional consequences. This chapter argues that managers in practice can deal with some of the problems of the imperfections of accounting measurement through the application of an interactive communicative method of coauthoring and a reflective learning model of truth.

Introduction[1]

One purpose of management accounting is to contribute to the performance management of the investment center managers of decentralized organizations (Solomon 1965; Anthony and Govindarajan 2007; Kaplan and Atkinson 2015). The governance of decentralized corporations involves the HQ-management transfer of decision-making

---

[1]The chapter contains excerpts that are "Reprinted from Nørreklit et al. (2006) with permission from Elsevier and from Nørreklit et al. (2017) with permission from Taylor and Francis Group LLC Books."

authority to investment center managers. For instance, consider the following case:

> A division sells a wide range of building materials to professional customers. The division consists of forty units organised as autonomous investment centres, each with its own local manager. Each investment centre is strategically restricted to its business area (products and market segments). Investments have to be approved by the HQ-management. But apart from that, each investment centre enjoys considerable freedom as regards sourcing, sales and marketing, product mix, and operational management (Nørreklit et al. 2006).

Outlined in the following is the principal–agent theory framework, which is the most common approach to the performance measurement of investment centers. Then, a contrasting approach based on pragmatic constructivism is presented.

Principal–Agent Theory

Principal–agent theory looks at the investment center managers as opportunistic agents with more information about alternative actions and their consequences than the principal, that is, the HQ manager (the so-called problem of asymmetric information; Kaplan and Atkinson 2015; Jensen and Meckling 1976). This constitutes the agency problem of moral hazard, that is, the question of how the agent is motivated to act in the interest of the principal. Due to the problem of moral hazard, a demand exists from the top management for information about the performance of the investment center management. The visibility of performance measurement should ensure the investment center manager is held accountable for their performance. This helps to ensure that the division manager has the motivation to pursue decision alternatives that are not only in their self-interest but also benefit the HQ management. A key issue is to ensure that the investment center manager produces credible information for the HQ's management planning and decision making.

Accounting measurement tools are, thus, seen as a mechanical instrument to govern the principal–agent relationship. Measuring the actual financial performance controllable by the agent and linking these results to the divisional manager's reward is suggested to be effective in motivating employees to work toward stated targets. Typically investment center managers are assumed to control sales, costs, and assets and can, therefore, be held accountable for financial figures, such as return on investment, assets, net assets, or equity (ROI, ROA, RONA, ROE) and economic value added (EVA). EVA is argued to be superior to the others because it does not take the cost of equity capital into account. The philosophy of EVA rate is that a company only creates value to its shareholder if the ROE is higher than the weighted average cost of capital (WACC). Thus, a proprietary and financially oriented set of performance measures are the tradition in this context.

In order to provide undistorted incentives, performance contracts for divisional managers should be constructed in such a way that the agent knows the desirable results and that the results are controllable and measurable in a quantitative and unequivocal way (Merchant 1985). However, in practice, this is a challenging task (Puxty 1985).

First, there is the inability to isolate the investment of the divisional manager's unique contributions to results. For example, different environmental conditions (technological, economic, political, etc.) and decisions and costs imposed by headquarters usually affect the performance of a subsidiary's operation. Therefore, accounting performance measures are usually distorted by noncontrollable factors, and, hence, it becomes impossible to provide performance measures that consist exclusively of factors controllable by the divisional manager. Also, these differences prevent a direct comparison of operations across divisions and in one division over time and so create ambiguity as to the appropriate performance norm.

Furthermore, there is an inability to measure financial results objectively. Accountants have traditionally advocated and used the system of historic cost accounting that, for much of its content, strives for a referential observational system that allows verification from past transaction records and documentation (i.e., original purchase costs and revenue recognition). However, a major problem of historical accounting figures is that the financial consequences of the uncompleted chains of action extend beyond the time of measurement. The historic cost accounting model implies that value measurement is restricted to assets that have been subject to factual transactions and hence ignores the wealth inherent in such factors as the creation of firm reputation, research in progress, and employee expertise and motivation. While it is a possibility that these types of attributes will have great value, they are not factual. Also, there are practical flexibilities concerning measurement issues (such as depreciation of fixed assets, valuation of stock, establishment of provisions, recognition of income, variation in the purchasing power of the measurement currency, and segregation of capital and revenue expenditures) that make it difficult to produce indisputable factual information (Sterling 1979; Chambers 1966). In addition, some of the measures involve the need to make future estimates, for example, assets' life, consumption patterns and residual values, debtor receipts, and stock selling prices. The distortion of historical accounting statements might be further aggravated by pressure on the divisional manager (whose rewards are linked to results) to produce ever-improving results. This can push the divisional manager to achieve short-term financial results rather than striving to make long-term investments in growth and innovation potential. Also, financial accountability controls may induce non–goal-congruent behavior (the opposite of their intention) and management myopia (Merchant 1985).

Some have advocated that the financial results' focus should be on income and asset value calculated on the basis of a net present value (NPV) approach, where evaluation is made on the basis of expectations about future cash flow. As future receipts must be anticipated or predicted and cannot, by definition, be measured, under this approach, manager's expectations or feelings about the future should be taken into consideration. In practice, this economics-based tradition does not meet any criterion of realism, and this is one of the reasons why it has been rejected for serving the stewardship role of financial accounting. Alternatively, the market view can enter financial accounting practice as a basis for determining income and value. It is argued to provide an objective point of reference for financial statements. However, when market price does not exist, a "fair value" surrogate has to be used. Fair value is about the estimation of a fair price from an orderly transaction between two parties at the date of measurement. Similar to economics-based values, market-based prices (including fair values) involve the recognition of unrealized income that may or may not translate into cash benefits for the stakeholder.

In view of the above, it is questionable where this mechanical instrumental approach to control is effective in the performance management of the managers of the investment centers. There is a need for developing methods for the performance management of investment centers in order to create more trustworthy knowledge. In the following, we outline an alternative framework for how organizations can structure their performance management of investment centers and incorporate management accounting information into it. We will demonstrate the framework by elaborating on the case introduced previously.

Pragmatic Constructivist Approach

Pragmatic constructivism is based on the assumption that managers in practice can deal with some of the problems of imperfectness in the production and use of accounting measurements through methods of coauthoring and by adopting a learning theory of truth (Nørreklit 2017; Nørreklit et al. 2010).

Coauthoring and Learning Theory of Truth

In practice, HQ management are unlikely to delegate all decision and action authority to the divisional manager. Thus, managers at both levels can be actors involved in *authoring* the activities of the centers, and, hence, they are co-actors in the creation of the investment center performance. More specifically, organizational practice is a factory of interwoven and interconnected narratives about local activities in which all the actors involved are constantly concerned with creating a local function narrative while simultaneously functioning together with others in coauthoring and, thereby creating, a coordinated set of actions representing functioning practice. Accounting numbers are produced that acquire meaning within specific narratives. Thereby, the principal–agent relationship might be formulated in a less oppositional manner and performance measurement might be used less instrumentally since it gets integrated with divisional managers' leadership process. For instance, in the case introduced previously,

> The HQ manager regularly meets with the local divisional centre managers several times each year. The meeting agenda includes items such as the debating of the plan, the follow-up of the plan, and the motivating of efficiency and performance. The communicative interaction between the HQ manager and the divisional manager takes the form of a dialogue. An overall strategy of the division forms the background knowledge for the meetings. It is revised and formulated every third year.

Managers of investment centers are actors (i.e., they take actions) who are the source of intentions and activities of organizational units. They mold and participate in the construction of the organization's value system and the activities in their investment center. Through communicative interaction and performance measurement, the HQ's management can influence the divisional investment center managers' intentions and activities and vice versa.

Also, in practice, the historical and future dimension of accounting might not be abruptly separated but rather integrated in a continuous observational process of proactive and pragmatic truths. In practice, measurements might be linked to narratives that are of holistic and reflective nature in order to get trustworthy meaning to the numbers below the surface levels. In particular, the interplay between pragmatic truth and proactive truth forms the basis for the ongoing improvement of the ability to generate historical and future-oriented accounting information and so establish an integrated learning-based theory of truth.

In the following, we illustrate how the HQ manager can engage in interactive communication and orchestrated interplay between pragmatic and proactive truths in the production and use of accounting models and information at both the HQ and the local divisional unit levels. Thus, in the organization, they work with the learning theory of truth in a broad range of activities, such as evaluation of local divisional managers' business performance, developing the performance measurement model, and production of accounting information.

Evaluating Local Managers' Business Performance

The division manager grounds a great deal of their total assessment in the local manager's past financial results. There are no bonuses linked to financial results, but it influences the negotiation of the following years' salary. Rather than getting a bonus, financially successful managers can look for new, although risky, possibilities that may create more value to the company. As most local managers like a high degree of autonomy, the HQ management motivates them to pursue their own values. However, their trust and confidence in the local managers' business models are proportional to the local manager's historical ability to generate sufficient profit. Overall, if an investment center is doing well, it will not get much attention; however, if a local manager is not performing, the HQ manager will intensify the dialogues with the local manager in an attempt to strengthen the business model. If a HQ manager is not able to mobilize the will and energy of the local manager to develop their own business models, then the HQ manager decides to let go the local manager.

Accordingly, the historical ability to meet profit targets may be used as a significant indication of the proactive truth of the local manager's business model. Hence, the ability to create pragmatic truth is used as an indication of proactive truth plans. However, planning and decision making involve the estimations of realistic expectations of future performance in order to facilitate arrangement of investments, overdraft, and other funding requirements and the acquisition at appropriate times of the volume of resources necessary to achieve the planned activity levels. As a great deal of accounting information does not hold over time and hence cannot be generalized over time, they need budgets. Therefore, there is a need to evaluate whether the budgets represent proactive truth.

When evaluating the proactive truth of the local managers' budget, the HQ manager analyses their business models, including their reflections on how to infer the activities necessary, to go from the existing reality construction to another future reality construction. Any reasoned or well-argued budget is based on valid business models, which implies that they have to express a solid understanding of the nature of integration in order to successfully guide organizational actions.

In validating the business models, the division manager assesses the proactive truth of the local managers' action plans and budgets. Their view is that budgets must be realistic. The targets are consciously set by the local managers at an achievable level (i.e., factually possible), while guarding against budget targets that are too optimistic or pessimistic. The HQ manager tries to assess the proactive truth of the budget data and plans for each local manager through a dialogical communication strategy that enables them to assess the integration of the local manager's business model.

In evaluating the factual possibility of the plan, the HQ manager tries to assess the factual basis and judgment behind the local manager's decisions and, in particular, to assess how confident they are in the integration embedded in their own plans. Especially in a situation in which the structure of the division includes autonomous investment centers, the assessment is critically important because responsibility and control have been decentralized. If the manager in charge of the center exercises poor judgment, it will, ceteris paribus, decrease the performance of his unit.

During budget meetings, the HQ manager listens to the local manager's budget proposal expressing values, possibilities, and factual conditions. Then, they challenge the proposal partly by disclosing the subjective judgment involved and partly through the negation of factual assumptions:

> When I meet with the local managers, they have described their plans and I ask them what they have not described. What are you afraid of? If there is a problem, I ask them what they feel like doing about it, and then they find the solution.

Thus, the HQ manager attempts to uncover the local manager's perception of the extent to which the budget reasoning will work in practice and, consequently, the extent to which facts, possibilities, and values are integrated. The HQ manager questions weak factual possibilities and value support in the plan. If there is a problem, the division manager's enquiries induce the local manager to find solutions that may negate the nonsupporting fact, weak possibilities, and values.

In applying their communication model, the HQ manager not only checks but also strengthens the judgment of the local manager and so improves the local manager's ability to control the center. Specifically, if the local manager is uncertain about how to create integration, then the HQ manager applies their communication strategy in an attempt to *encourage* the local manager to find ways to build integration.

In addition, for the evaluation of the realism of the budget (moral hazard) the HQ manager assesses the extent to which the factual possibilities embedded in the external conditions of a particular investment center fit the organizational objectives. Interpreting the numbers requires an experienced and knowledgeable manager who can assess the results of the units in a particular context. To be able to follow developments and interpret the figures, the manager's subjective knowledge and insights about the units being assessed is important.

Previously, we revealed an interactive narrative that forms the basis for cooperative managers' reflective evaluation and learning processes concerning the manager of the investment centers' business strategy and actions. The HQ manager uses both historically based accounting information and future-oriented accounting estimations as elements in a more complex knowledge and judgment system including methods for assessing both the proactive truth and pragmatic truths of local manager's business models. A truth gap gives rise to an intensive learning process driven by the HQ manager.

Performance Measurement Model

Also, the HQ manager works with a learning theory of truth in the development of performance measurement ratios. Fundamentally, to provide useful accounting information, a performance measurement system should be designed to serve the purpose (intentional value) it has in the reality construction. The conceptual items of accounting measurement models are outlined by the formulation of conceptual content and criteria that are exemplar and structurally linked together through logical relationships. As logic cannot be positively observed, their truth cannot be found by empirical correspondence. It is only through reflective reasoning in relation to the specific practice that accounting models such as historical versus economic value model and ROI versus EVA can be assessed in terms of their usefulness in the real world. The interplay between pragmatic truth and proactive truth forms the basis for an ongoing improvement of the model in use.

In our case, the financial objective of the organization is to produce the highest ROI in the industry and to have "balanced" financing of their growth. Aiming to serve these objectives, the investment centers are measured on the basis of a blend of EVA and RONA. Thus, their profits are calculated after deducting 1 percent interest per month on the invested working capital. The hurdle rate of ROI required is a minimum of 14 percent. But in fact some units have a rate of return of 40 percent while others have less than 14 percent. Rates above 14 percent are considered positively, while rates below 14 percent are considered a danger. In addition, the division requires 40 percent of gross profits for personnel costs—this percentage depends on whether the yard has its own transportation company. Also, the market share and the monthly turnover rate of accounts receivable and stocks are measured.

Prior to the introduction of this system, the ROI was used. The new system of calculating profits after the reduction of interest on working capital was developed some years ago. The reason was that some of the investment centers exploited the fact that they could get higher interest from their debtors than ROI. Debtors were a very real problem, and some of the investment centers suffered substantial losses because of this situation. The hurdle rate implies that there is no incentive to pursue alternatives with returns lower than the cost of capital. The organization does not use the full EVA, as they do not want the local managers to promote investments that go to close to the border of WACC.

Overall, we witness that the top management aims to develop a model that fits the purpose and that there is managerial reflection on the pragmatic effect of the model.

Financial Statements

Finally, it should be noted that the learning theory of truth governs the production of numbers in financial accounting reporting. The financial reports are made based on the standards and principles of financial accounting.

The conceptual system of financial accounting is used to measure managers' performance.

Generally, in practice, historical accounting information builds on the interplay between proactive truth and pragmatic truth. Consequently, historic cost accounting's limitations as an objective referential observational system might not be so much a problem in practice. Rather, it is crucial for trustworthiness in accounting to ascertain whether the referent is real or illusionary. To be real, financial accounting statements should integrate all the four dimensions of pragmatic constructivism. Many, but not all, of the contents of historic cost–based financial statements are based on references to factual financial transactions. However, these are not objective or physical facts, but facts based on constructs integrated with the possibilities and human values that determine their selection. Financial statements are based on what has been factually possible to do. Much of the linking to possibilities is historically based; for example, inventory is based on historical evidence of its existence and that it has been factually possible to produce a certain item at a certain historic cost. Some of the measures in financial statements involve the need to make future estimates, for example, assets' life, consumption patterns and residual values, debtor receipts, and stock selling prices. Thus, historical reporting is also based on what is assumed to be factually possible to do. The use of future information inevitably makes accounting information moderately subjective. However, to make the numbers trustworthy, accounting practices draw on the elements of proactive and pragmatic truths when making judgments. Thus, guiding the subjective judgment in financial statements are principles of going concern, conservatism, consistency, and reliability. For example, evaluations of debtor receipts and stock selling prices are reflectively based on a judgment of whether the debtors will pay and whether the goods in stock will sell for that price. The proactive judgment is an integrated part of a pragmatic observation of whether debtors are paying and stock is selling. In this way, the assumptions about what may be factually possible to do and values to be employed in reporting are linked to the conservative projections of historically rooted business.

In our case, the willingness and factual possibilities of customers' ability to pay are checked proactively at the order stage, and, after delivery, debtors are controlled tightly. More specifically, they have a credit maximum, so that debtors of more than a certain amount are referred to the HQ manager. The HQ manager approves debtors who are of acceptable financial status, that is, those who proactively seem to be able and willing to pay. For everybody else, the local manager has to give a trustworthy explanation for selling to such customers. Also, the HQ manager checks that the company's policies are followed and that the debtors are actually paying. For example, they regularly check the debtors of the investment centers, and any center with unapproved or problematic debtors has to submit an explanation. In this way, they manage to get the debtors under control. As a matter of fact, they have been able to reduce the accounts receivable turnover rate from the average credit period of 105 days down to 36 days.

Similarly, the HQ manager ensures that buildings are not neglected. During the meetings, the HQ manager examines the state of the buildings and stores. In addition, the people who evaluate the condition of the buildings sometimes also attend the meetings.

Thus, although in a dynamic business context historically based conservative information might be considered misleading in respect of what is factually possible and valuable in the future, it might provide a solid foundation for the proactive judgment of the effect of operational actions or nonactions.

Conclusions

Earlier in this chapter, we discussed how a HQ manager engaged in reflective communicative interaction with local managers about past and future business actions. The top management did not handover all the authority to the center managers to determine what to do; instead, they created a climate of co-actorship in the creation of the investment center performance. The proactive and pragmatic evaluation of the integration of the local managers' business models is crucial when the HQ manager validates the local manager's actions. The production and use of trustworthy and meaningful accounting information and methods is a focal point in narrating this evaluation. The interplay between pragmatic truth and proactive truth information forms the basis for an ongoing improvement of the ability to generate historical and future-oriented accounting information and so establish an integrated learning-based theory of truth.

Accordingly, pragmatic constructivism provides a basis for the performance management of investment centers that is rather different from the instrumental and mechanical leadership style embedded in the principal–agent theory that currently dominates the conventional wisdom on the performance management of investment centers.

Discussion Questions

1. How does the principal–agent theory relate to the four dimensions of pragmatic constructivism (facts, possibilities, values, and communication)? What are the blind spots of integration embedded in the principal–agent theory thinking?

2. Drawing on pragmatic constructivism, you are asked to design a performance management system for a divisionalized organization! What measures will you suggest? How will you validate the quality of the information? How will you use the accounting information?

CHAPTER 7

Strategic Performance Management

Falconer Mitchell, Hanne Nørreklit, Lars Braad Nielsen, and Lennart Nørreklit

Insights from This Case Study

A company's financial end-result performance is determined by two interrelated factors: operational performance and strategic performance. The aggregate measurement of the two types of performance implies that there is a lack of observation of the management's strategic performance. This chapter articulates a conceptual meaning and tools for strategic performance measurement. Drawing on pragmatic constructivism, strategy is conceptualized to be about creating and enacting an overarching business model that aims to create strategic coherence among groups of operating actors over time. Strategic performance measurement involves an ex ante evaluation of whether the strategic narrative will be able to succeed (proactive truth) and ex post reflections as to whether the strategy was successful (pragmatic truth). Such function of strategic performance measurement presupposes that the strategy is formulated and the ongoing feedback created by the monitoring system forms the basis of strategic managerial learning.

Introduction[1]

The purposes of this chapter are to articulate a conceptual meaning for strategic performance measurement as a leadership tool and to identify a conceptual framework for its development. It is perceived as a means of

---

[1]The chapter contains excerpts that are "Reprinted from Mitchell et al. 2013 with permission from Springer."

not only assessing leadership performance but also as a basis of providing constructive feedback that will enable improvements to be made in strategic performance.

The chapter takes as its starting point the need to distinguish strategic performance from operational performance and some external influences on organizational performance. Exhibit 7.1, although in itself a simplification of reality, illustrates the complexities of this task. End-result performance is determined by a number of interrelated factors, one of which is strategic performance. Thus, the end result may be improved by good strategic performance. However, there may also be a good (or bad) end result, despite poor (or good) strategic performance as a consequence of the positive (or negative) influence of all or any of the other influential factors. Accordingly, in this analysis end-result measures are, at best, regarded as partial or incomplete indicators of the quality of strategic performance. To provide reliable leadership assessment and feedback, conceptions of good (or poor) strategic performance therefore require to be made independently of end-result performance (Mitchell et al. 2013).

The lack of observation of the management's strategic performance in the dominant strategic performance measurement models implies that the models can neither contribute to assessing top management performance or improving its strategic decision-making capability. This is problematic as there are large amounts of money involved at the strategic level. It is important for any organization to be aware of whether the issues faced are of operational nature or strategic nature. Within certain limits, top executives can always try to put operational results in the place of strategic performance. If the strategic performance is poor, extraordinary pressure on operational activities can compensate for a failing strategy. Thus, there is a need for a strategic performance measurement tool that can be used to assess the strategic performance of the top executives and to provide constructive feedback to improve management's strategic practices.

Mainstream literature on strategic performance measurement focuses on helping top management when implementing company strategies and policies (Kaplan and Norton 1996; Nørreklit 2000). The models imply that strategic goals and activities are formulated by the senior management and then translated into performance targets for managers and employees at the operational levels. Feedback information is concerned with the implementation of strategy at the operational level but is silent about the ability of top management in formulating a robust strategy. Techniques for analyzing the strategic performance of top management are thus underdeveloped in the models.

Exhibit 7.1

Strategic performance in situ

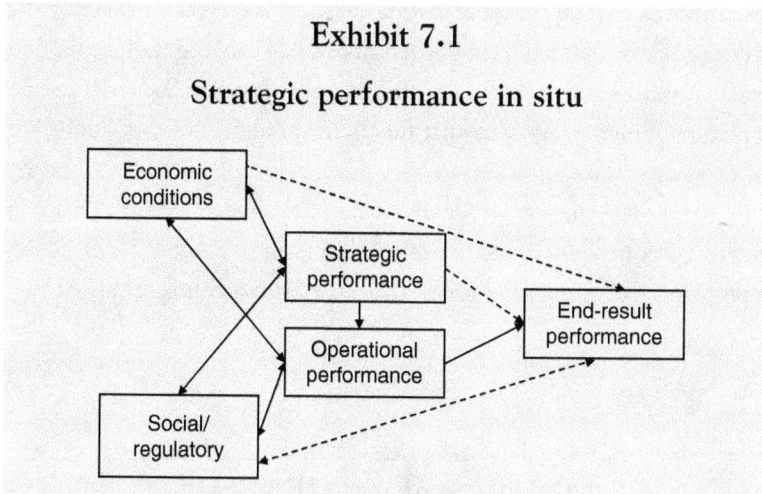

The chapter is structured as follows. First, pragmatic constructivism is employed to identify the nature and purpose of strategic performance. Second, key information concepts upon which systems of strategic performance measurement can be built are outlined. Finally, some conclusions are drawn and ideas are presented.

Strategic Performance

When defining strategic performance, we consider the notion of strategic fit in the context of pragmatic constructivism coherence, which underlies most of the dominating strategic literature as a vital concept for company performance (Chandler 1962/1998; Miles and Snow 1978; Heijltjes 1995). It is stated that strategy is concerned with creating a match between a company's external business conditions (market demands, competitors, suppliers, institutions, regulations, etc.) and its internal structures that constitute chain of activities and resources (R&D, manufacturing, logistic, sales and marketing, etc.). Strategic coherence is a quality of these relationships, which enables the company to operate effectively in creating and meeting environmental expectations and achieve numerical results. Lack of coherence creates chaos, and things become unpredictable because the activities have conflicting consequences and therefore destroy each other.

The overall strategic task of top management is therefore to develop the strategic profile that results in the best fit possible between the internal and external factors and, hence, high strategic performance. Society is itself a structure of high complexity that functions through endless relationships of coherence, constantly driven by coherency problems to be solved by companies and other activity centers. The company has to find its place in the complex network of relationships of coherency. Exhibit 7.2 illustrates a problem of coherence in the case of a large Danish company, HEALTH.

Exhibit 7.2

Case of coherence problems in the Danish company, HEALTH

HEALTH is a large Danish company with approximately 7,000 employees selling products and services to people with medical problems in more than 60 countries. Core competences and technologies are developed around the value of making life easier for people with a particular illness. In cooperation with professional health personnel, new products are developed that provide high-quality services that meet the individual user's special needs. In addition, sustainable profitability is a core value. The customers are very conservative and tend to continue to use the product they leave the hospital with. Therefore, the health personnel's product recommendations are important for future sales.

The company is structured around four main executive areas: *global R&D*, with the responsibility of developing new products and services; *global operations*, comprising all manufacturing activities along with the logistics and the design, assembly, and technical maintenance of machinery; *global marketing*, with the primary responsibility of obtaining market information and developing strategies for future product launches; and *sales region* focusing on sales and customer services worldwide. Over the years, the organization has been reconstructing the pattern of coherence to reestablish the effectiveness by reshaping the chain of operating units and aiming at solving new coherence issues in the market.

For instance, in the beginning of the 2000s, a coherence problem arose between the company's external business condition and its internal manufacturing activities due to fierce global competition implying that labor costs in Denmark are higher compared to many other possible manufacturing locations. Therefore, to increase coherence around the dimension of cost efficiency with its environment, the organization decided to offshore some manufacturing facilities to Hungary and China. Therefore, today, manufacturing in HEALTH takes place at its facilities in Denmark and in Hungary and China. As such, the production facilities in Denmark—known as *technical competence centers*—are primarily intended for the research and testing of new products on a small scale requiring the design and assembly of prototype machinery. Once product development has been completed and the production processes have been thoroughly tested, production is normally moved to China or Hungary and increased in scale. This has created another coherence problem.

First, they have had to consider new types of coherence problems in relation to manufacturing competences and output quality. Thus, it takes a very long time to build up sufficient skills and competences in a manufacturing plant. When starting a new factory, they physically moved experienced employees from one established factory to another, so they lived in a new location and worked for a year at the new factory. The standard products were also moved from one established factory to another to facilitate the transition from pilot production to full-scale manufacturing.

Furthermore, when they develop a new product, they design the machinery and tools and start the manufacturing in Denmark. And when the product is matured, the manufacturing is moved to Hungary. But those people who are designing the machinery and maturing the product are employees who have been in the company for 10 to 20 years.

(continued)

And they are designing the tools and maturing the manufacturing process because they have been working around the machinery for many years. In 10 years, additional staff came on board but they have never been around designing the machines and maturing the product. This led to a competence dilution at the Denmark facility, and the company became very concerned about getting the diluted competences replaced with matching competence and competence building in China and Hungary.

Coherence can be analyzed at different organizational levels. At the operational level, there is the coherence between specific chains of activities. Within the operative units, integration of the four dimensions is controlled by specialized, professional way of reasoning. The integration within the operational units is the condition for the creation of construct causality and for the activities to be performed successfully. The coherence between the functional units is a result of the merger of overall operational planning with strategic performance to create the internal–external fit; therefore, it is the strategic coherence when seen from a top-down perspective in the company. The development of strategic coherence concentrates on practical aspects of creating an overarching form of construct causality throughout the whole value chain to make a set of interrelated ways of reasoning running the company successfully together. Specifically within the Danish company HEALTH, the development of strategic coherence relates to connecting the functions of R&D, manufacturing, and marketing and sales. The functional departments are all integrated around their individual ways of reasoning, and, thus, coherence is to be viewed as the ability to create an overarching business model that aims to make the specialized departmental ways of reasoning to create construct causality in interaction with their environment.

In order to establish overall coherence between all operating units of the company and its environment, strategic leadership aims at creating strategic coherence between operating units through the creation of strings of output–demand relationships. Essentially, strategic coherence is closely tied to effectiveness. While efficiency measures the degree of input–output target fulfillment in operational activities, effectiveness indicates the degree to which the operational activity output meets the overall company goals. Thus, operational performance is linked to efficiency and the relationship between input and output, while strategic performance is linked to effectiveness and the relationship between output and company goals. An organization is a complex mix of activities, each of which can be seen as an operation that transforms input into output that should subsequently help meet the company goals. In coordination between the operating units, the output of one unit is to be coherent with the demand of another unit. For instance, in HEALTH, the service output of product development and design activities has to meet the demand of manufacturing and sales. When using effectiveness as a performance measure, it is pivotal to distinguish between the goal and the purpose of the output. The purpose of the output is to fulfill the need of the next operating unit in the chain. The goal is a relevant measure of effectiveness only if it expresses the need of the receiving unit. Accordingly, the objective that is relevant to effectiveness is not a function of planning as such but of the needs of the receiver of the output.

The coherence between parties, in the market (e.g., companies) as well as within the company (e.g., departments), must occur across four dimensions: facts, possibilities, values, and communication. Coherence does not mean that the facts, possibilities, and values of the interacting parties must be identical but rather that they must complement each other. Coherence should be expressed conceptually in the communication that connects the units. The value is whether the recipient actually wants to use the delivered service. The factual possibility issue is whether it is able to deliver the number of output products and services that are capable of doing things needed by the recipient. Finally, communication is concerned with the recipient's ability to explain and understand the service delivered. Failure of coherence may simply be an issue of misunderstanding, because the units speak different languages; for instance, production may describe the product in a technical way of reasoning that differs from the ways of reasoning used by sales staff and customers. For instance, in HEALTH, the strategy is formulated around fulfilling the needs of people with a particular illness and the value of efficient manufacturing processes. Among others, the internal coherence of R&D activities with the external market request relates to whether R&D can and will develop such a product. Thus, it should be factually possible for R&D to develop a product that meets the demand and the R&D personnel should have values that motivate them to develop such a product. Finally, they should be able to participate in communicative interaction with other units to explain and understand the service they have delivered to other units.

When strategic coherence across the four dimensions is not in place, top management must seek to reconstruct the pattern of coherence in order to reestablish the effectiveness by reshaping the chain of operating units and aiming at solving new coherence issues in the market. In a short-term perspective, strategic activities can accept certain incoherencies in present operations in order to create new structures that display higher degrees of coherency. Accordingly, strategy must maintain and improve coherence over a long-term perspective. The need for integration of multidimensional ways of reasoning across time implies that the establishment and measurement of strategic coherence between operating units are highly dynamic and complex matters.

Overall, the strategy is concerned with developing an overarching integrated way of reasoning that is able to create coherence by bridging the specialized ways of reasoning of the cooperating units. The relationship between the delivered service and the demand itself constitutes the cooperation of larger integrated units. Strategic performance relates to establishing best possible *coherence* between the ways of reasoning of the external environment and internal operations. The strategic performance of a given period is represented by the actions carried out to improve the strategic coherence of the company–environment relationship. Accordingly, managerial strategic performance reflects the changes in the strategic situation, that is, the changes in the coherence of the strategic profile that take place over a certain period of time.

Strategic Performance Measurement

Strategic performance measurement assumes the ability of management to formulate a realistic strategy; it is a system of implementing and monitoring the achievement of the strategy and learning and revising the strategy (Asch 1992; Simons 1995). Strategic performance measurement that is applied to drive strategic performance therefore involves an ex ante evaluation of whether the intended strategy will be able to succeed (proactive truth) and ex post reflections as to whether the strategy was successful (pragmatic truth). Such a function of strategic performance measurement presupposes that the strategy is formulated and the ongoing feedback created by the monitoring system forms the basis of strategic managerial learning.

In the following, we describe the key dimensions for constructing a strategic performance measurement system that involves the formulation of a strategic planning narrative, evaluation of whether the narrative is proactive truth, methods of measuring change in strategic coherence, and a learning theory of truth.

Strategic Planning Narrative

To organize the strategic process consciously, leaders have to formulate a narrative of the strategy for their managers and employees to know what to do and what to expect. The narrative should be able to explain the issues in relation to developing an overarching integrated way of reasoning in order to bridge the gaps between specialized ways of reasoning of the cooperating units over time. Therefore, it needs to include a description of the intentional future situations in which the main functions of strategic focus at that time have to be coherent and the strategic method saying something about the present situation and how to move from the present to the future situation. To strategically connect units that are driven by different specialized ways of reasoning and, therefore very different conceptual logics, is a complex cognitive process that involves developing an overarching way of reasoning that is understood and accepted by all interacting units.

The strategic narrative formulation also includes an outline of the general structure of goals and activities that function as basis for the specific goal setting in operational planning (see Exhibit 7.3). Thus, based on the strategic narrative, a system of goals connecting the operating units can be formulated. Goal setting is a planning instrument that aims to influence the operating units to coordinate the output–need relationship and enable effectiveness. There are two performance issues in goal setting: the ability to fulfill the goal (implementation) and the purpose of the goal (ability to fulfill the need). The executing operating unit prefers goals that can be implemented efficiently, while the receiving operating unit prefers goals that serve its needs so that it can function efficiently. In this way, goal setting related to effectiveness is a process of mediation between operating units to create a coherent system of goals. Hence, even though specific goals are established through operational planning, they are guided by the overall system of goals established by strategic perform-ance management. Also, the goal formulation must be subjected to per-formance evaluation. This assumes that there are performance targets for the organizational unit determined independently of the defined goals. The set of goals can and should be formulated and monitored to form a control mechanism of the strategic planning. Measurement can indicate the degree of targeted coherence achieved.

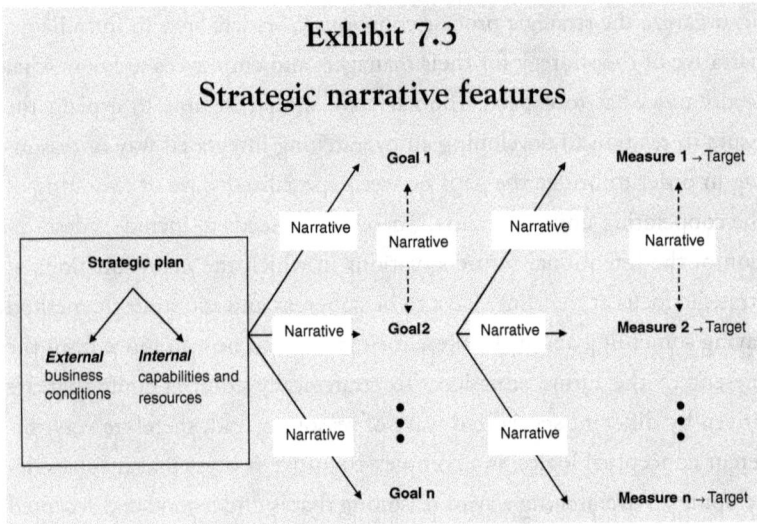

Exhibit 7.3

Strategic narrative features

The formulation of a coherent strategic narrative that connects goals across specialized organizational units with multiple actors' intentionality and strategic methods involves a management process of coauthorship and, hence, an actor-based approach. Here, the formulation process is organized in such a way that the organizational actors participate as link-ing pins in the goal formulation effort of the top management. The for-mulation process is initiated from the top, but the interaction among the various constituencies involved takes place as a dialogue. On one hand, this gives the multiple operational actors a bottom-up opportunity to contribute to the goal formulation process. On the other, the top management through its communicative processes influences their subordinates' intentional values and cultivation of strategic methods.

Proactive Truth of the Narrative

The first and basic evaluation of strategic performance concerns the quality and implementation of strategic narratives. The focal point is whether together they can create construct causality. The evaluation assesses the understanding, acceptance, and evaluation of the proactive truth of the narrative by the different unit leaders involved. A unit leader may for instance experience a narrative as fiction, irrelevant, impossible to implement, or as a poor interpretation of the possibilities and values of the company. A new strategy may be destructive for the efficiency of a unit, and the degree and duration of such effects must be taken into consideration. For instance, in HEALTH, the strategy of establishing manufacturing competences capable of meeting the output objectives might not be factually possible and might become counterproductive for R&D's ability to create new products. The narrative may be biased because it is based on input from a few dominating leaders disregarding other leaders whose units are of equal importance. For the narrative to function, it should be subject to an open dialogue in which the concerns of the various units can be taken into account. This can be uncovered by an analysis of the formulation and acceptance of the strategic narrative by the unit leaders. Furthermore, the strategic narrative must reflect trends in various environments, for example, technological development, market demands, and so on. This can also be analyzed by having a qualified analyst interview the strategic leadership. An overall evaluation of the credibility of strategic narrative is whether it reflects and integrates the factual possibilities and values concerned as well as be able to function in communicative interaction with other units.

Measuring Changes in Strategic Coherence

The next step in strategic performance measurement is to create indicators to measure the coherence between the units connected directly by output–demand relationships. Strategic performance measurement requires information about the strategic performance related to the different operational units of the company and the flows between them as well as between these units and the market and institutional environment. Since the operating units create a chain of coherent links, it is possible to trace problems indicated at one place to other places in the chain from where they may originate. To obtain such traceability in the implementation of the linking goals, qualitative and quantitative performance measures can be applied to shed light on the achievement of the various aspects of the strategic goals outlined. The narrative and goal formulation play a crucial role in reasoning and justifying the specific choice of performance targets and measures.

Monitoring of changes in coherence can be used to reflect on the adequacy of the strategy to establish construct causality and to adjust the strategic behavior and thereby improve company's performance in future. Accordingly, strategic measurement requires indicators that directly reflect changes in coherence. Therefore, to observe the internal–external fit, one may install a measurement of any output–goal link between operating units at any point of time. This establishes a measurement system that allows the leadership to monitor changes in the degree of coherence and thus guide strategic activities aiming at making incremental improvements in the internal relationships in an ongoing manner. The effects of new strategic goals on the operational efficiency of the units have to be taken into account. Therefore, it is vital to create a performance evaluation system that is based on analyses of some or all the various links of coherence in the system. Coherency goals can be formulated for each of these links to motivate the implementation of strategic coherence, and measurements of goal fulfillment may be used as drivers for the ongoing improvement of strategic performance by constantly incentivizing cooperating units' learning how to create strategic coherence.

For this purpose, we suggest using real-time measurements of coherence issues. Thus, there is absolutely no need to use ex ante and ex post measurements to estimate the overall performance. Instead, measurements can be installed as real-time information systems that enable managers to estimate how they perform strategically during the process. The measurement system thus becomes a learning device and motivator for the strategic process. This constitutes a measurement of the implementation of the strategic idea in the company, that is, the internal coherence of the functions of the company activities. The real-time measurement of change in the strategic profile makes it possible to trace the problems to their various sources in two aspects: the place where the problem originates and the un-integrated dimension(s) that stops strategic action from taking place. Thus, it provides a basis for the assessment of strategic performance that enables the formulation of goals to drive the improvement of strategic profile.

We suggest the construction of an information platform that functions as the instrument for strategic performance measurement and learning. The platform may consist of a set of strategic scorecards, one each for the coherence relationships essential for the overall chain of activities and functions underpinning company's performance. Each scorecard analyzes the degree of coherence between units in the performance chain. In case of coherence problems, the card breaks down the information with respect to the dimensions that must be integrated for the relationship to be coherent. For instance, was the problem caused by insufficient information or a clash of values or by the lack of factual possibilities? The platform contains a top-level integration scorecard that reflects the change in the strategic profile of the company, that is, changes in the internal–external fit. For each of the links between internal units, an integration scorecard is constructed to reflect the changes in coherence between the units. If operational problems in an operating unit are caused or influenced by the output from another operating unit then those problems must be recorded in the integration scorecard as a coherence problem. Each scorecard contains qualitative data concerning the strategic narrative as it is perceived in the units and quantitative measurements related to the strategic coherency goals connecting the units involved. Exhibit 7.4 sketches an overall strategic scorecard of HEALTH. It provides an overview of the strategic expectation and reality.

Analyses of coherence in the system of links can be used to identify problems and their causes by *tracing coherence* problems, that is, tracing the signs of incoherence in one operating unit back to their causes in other parts of the system. If one does not trace the problems to their origins they cannot be eliminated. Thus, a system of coherency tracing is a fundamental tool to improve strategic coherence. The analysis of such chains of causality connections enables the formulation of goals and measurements that can resolve coherency problems and thus improve overall strategic coherence.

Exhibit 7.4

Strategic scorecard of HEALTH

Value chain (HEALTH)	Strategic expectation (i) Reductive narratives and goals	Strategic reality (ii) Performance measures	Strategic reflection (iii) Problems of coherence (integration and coherence tracing)
Market	Stable growth in the number of people with a particular illnesses, health care personnel influence users' first choice, vulnerable and conservative users, global labor market, products subsidized by government	Market shares, share of first users leaving the hospital with HEALTH products, superior product quality, governmental subsidizing, competitive manufacturing labor costs	Change in relative quality, change in relationship with health care professionals
Sales and marketing	Stable growth in sales, good relationship with health care personnel, good knowledge about market and understanding of users' needs	Sales growth, price, margin, sales mix, forecast accuracy	Forecast inaccuracy
Manufacturing and logistics	Automatic technology, flexible semiautomatic manufacturing equipment for some start-up, reliable manufacturing process, zero product-quality failure, effective delivery, competitive labor costs, reduction of waste, motivated workforce	Delivery gaps, back orders, late delivery, errors, development in skills and competences in new manufacturing plants, employee motivation	Competence problems

Value chain (HEALTH)	Strategic expectation (i) Reductive narratives and goals	Strategic reality (ii) Performance measures	Strategic reflection (iii) Problems of coherence (integration and coherence tracing)
R&D and engineering	Knowledge, capabilities, and motivation to make product innovation within core values Innovation in interaction with health care professionals and manufacturing and sales personnel Increase in the competences and capabilities in Hungary for designing tools and maturing of manufacturing	Action time, product problems, and failed projects Cost of overqualified employees	Dilution of competences in Denmark
Finance	Sustainable growth and profit; profit/cash generation; capital availability	Gearing, ROE, cash flow	Decrease in gearing

Strategic Truth Gap and Learning

In order to promote strategic learning, the strategic scorecard should be used to analyze the truth gap. A large gap implies poor strategic performance in the sense that strategic plans are not realized. This analysis is therefore motivated by the drive to reduce this gap, which means the ability to control the strategic situation through strategic behavior improves. Thus, part of the strategic performance is to ensure strategic control, which includes the reliability of the measurements used in the integration scorecards and, thus, the very goal setting that interprets the strategic narrative.

In a strategic context, where changing conditions are an essential part of performance, the notion of proactive and pragmatic truths is important. Pragmatic truth consequently means that the proposition is true if the operations that implement the expectations do succeed. A problem with this pragmatic concept of truth is that one can only know the truth after events have taken place. Since it is absurd to wait for ex post testing of strategic statements, a concept of preliminary, or proactive, truth is needed to provide a basis for action. This proactive truth is then subjected to a continuous process of improvement that identifies and diminishes the difference, or truth gap, in the pragmatic truth (i.e., the outcome). The truth gap between what we expected to do and what we did includes two dimensions: strategy setting and strategy execution. The deviation between what we should have done and what we did is the gap in strategic execution. The deviation between what we expected to do and what we should have done is the gap in strategy setting. The truth gap is to be kept small and insignificant. If it is large, information that is only proactively true can mislead users.

To enhance information reliability the truth gap must be monitored. The truth gap is likely to grow unless the apparatus creating proactive truth is improved on an ongoing basis. Increases in the truth gap must be traced to their origins in neglected coherency issues, new influences, and previously unobserved data. Thus, truth gap monitoring becomes a basis for a continuous learning and improvement process. Without this learning, proactive truth is likely to lose reliability. Especially in the dynamic situations of modern business, success requires not only the measurement of existing strategic performance but also the use of the learning process to devise and implement new strategies. Overall, it forms the basis for focused strategic reflection. The coherence measurements suggest functions as drivers not only because they can be used to motivate but also because they become learning devices since real-time monitoring of truth gap makes it possible to pinpoint the activities that actually reduce the truth gap.

Conclusions

This chapter has outlined a conceptual basis for the derivation of strategic performance measurement to be used for assessing the strategic performance of top executives and to provide constructive feedback to improve management's strategic practices. It is argued that strategic performance measurements should focus on issues of strategic coherence in relation to the pursuit and achievement of goals. Identifying the extent of coherence attained and ensuring that it is maintained and incrementally improved in the long term are taken as the prime aims of strategic management. To achieve this, the strategy adopted should also be valid and the measurement system adopted should support the validity of the means by which coherence is pursued. The achievement of validity in this sense requires strategic performance measurement to be based on a carefully constructed knowledge base or information platform specific to the internal and external circumstances of each organization. The generation of this intelligence base and its use to promote strategic coherence must involve the integration of facts, possibilities, values, and communication within and across the subunits of the organization and at the interfaces of the organization with its environment. Through its ongoing identification of strategic shortcomings, this approach is also designed to support strategic learning and improvement.

Discussion Questions

1. Drawing on pragmatic constructivism, evaluate the strengths and weaknesses of the balanced scorecard? How does balanced scorecard relate to the four dimensions of pragmatic constructivism (facts, possibilities, values, and communication)? What are the blind spots of integration embedded in the balanced scorecard? What might be the strategic consequences of the blind spots?

2. Drawing on pragmatic constructivism, you are asked to design a strategic performance management system for an organization! How will you orchestrate the production of a strategic scorecard? How will you produce the strategic scorecard? What measures will you suggest? How will you use the strategic scorecard?

CHAPTER 8

Operational Performance Management

Falconer Mitchell, Hanne Nørreklit, and Mihaela Trenca

Insights from This Case Study

The conventional thinking on the performance management of operational responsibility centers is dominated by the ideas of cybernetic and result controls. However, scholarly research and anecdotal evidence points to measurement challenges and dysfunctional implications of result control. Drawing on pragmatic constructivism, this chapter argues that the dysfunctional problems of operational performance measurement can to a certain extent be handled by the way the result measures are formulated and used. We present an actor-based method to the use of operational performance measurement. The method is illustrated through the case of an American supply chain manager. Core elements of the actor-based method are the manager's creation of a factual observational ground, management of employees' motivational values, orchestration of proactive, true problem solving, and observation of pragmatic truth and learning.

Introduction[1]

In this chapter, we explore the performance measurement of responsibility centers at the operational level. In operational responsibility centers, there are organizational managers who control either sales or expenses.

---

[1] The chapter contains excerpts that are "Reprinted from Trenca and Nørreklit (2017) with permission from Taylor and Francis Group LLC Books."

These managers are thus held responsible for profit performance that reflects their spectrum of control over revenues and expense measures. For the performance management of such operational centers result controls can be established through measurement targets or standards. In what follows, we explain the conventional approach to measuring the performance of operational units of manufacturing and sales and marketing. Subsequently, we discuss a pragmatic constructivist view of producing and using performance measures in this context.

Financial and Nonfinancial Measures

The conventional approach to performance measures of cost or expenditure aspects focuses on production efficiency (labor and material), price variance, and flexible budget variances. For the performance measurement of sales and marketing units focus is on revenue variance, sales price variances, contribution margins, product mix, and market share variances. However, in relation to the measurement of financial performance of these units there are problems with identifying the primary characteristic that serves as a pointer to the effective performance of those responsible for operational management. Thus, the principal does not know the right norm for results, and the results are not controllable and measurable in a quantitative and unequivocal way (Merchant 1985). Also, these performance measures might induce actions that are not congruent with the overall corporate objectives. There can be many factors that come into play (in addition to managerial actions) in a financial performance measure. The repetitive uncovering of dysfunctional behaviors such as suboptimization, short-term thinking, gaming, and measurement fixation exposes this shortcoming (Anthony and Govindarajan 2007; Kaplan and Atkinson 2015; Merchant and Van der Stede 2012).

In order to minimize these limitations, it has been suggested that financial measures be supplemented with nonfinancial measurement. For instance, for manufacturing units, nonfinancial performance measures within the following areas have been suggested: quality control measures, material control measures, inventory control measures, machine performance measurement, and delivery control measurement. Also, nonfinancial performance measures for important and indirect functions such as engineering have been suggested. For the performance measurement of sales and marketing units, various customer- and market-related measures have been pointed out. Some measures can focus on output targets while others are process-oriented measures monitoring the execution of throughput processes that are important for the achievement of targets. The measures should not be viewed as static standards but as evidence of a trend toward ideal goals. However, the inclusion of nonfinancial measures might also lead to dysfunctional behavior. In addition, it becomes a challenge to weight the various measures.

Overall, conventional thinking on performance measurement tends to see operational managers and employees as adaptors of norms. Indeed, managers and employees need direction, and performance measures can be an important mechanism in this regard. But from the perspective of pragmatic constructivism, when adapting to norms, managers and employees become actors, and the underlying actions they take to fulfill the norms might be dysfunctional for the organization. Driven by their intentionality, the organizational actor creates and controls activities in interaction with the situational context to achieve the intentional outcome. As management by numbers links achievement to reward, it connects the individual managers to extrinsic motivational values and not to their intrinsic motivational values. However, for responsible, creative, and reflective problem solving, it is paramount that the organizational objectives be connected to the actor's intrinsic motivational values. Often, in economic and managerial thinking intrinsic motives are greatly underrated, yet a large risk stems from the fact that intrinsic and extrinsic motives interact: Extrinsic motives drive out intrinsic motives.

The pragmatic constructivism approach suggests that the dysfunctional problems identified by operational performance measurement can, to a certain extent, be handled by the way performance measures are formulated and used. This will be further explained in the following two sections.

Operational Performance Measures

Pragmatic constructivism subscribes to the mainstream view that the operational measures should be linked to organizational strategy formulated at the top level. Standard textbooks (Anthony and Govindarajan 2007; Kaplan and Atkinson 2015) within the area of management accounting propose the implementation of performance measures in a hierarchical top-down manner. But these texts neither take into account individual perceptions and thinking of what is factually possible nor their emotions, intuition, and values. Mainly employees are perceived as a component in a system whose role is to serve the interests of the whole system, that is, the company.

But in a dynamic and complex business context there exists local situated knowledge for performance measurement (Trenca and Nørreklit 2017). Therefore, it is important to engage individual managers at all levels to take responsibility for the relevance of measures. Thus, a company is composed of multiple constituencies. The vertical perspective of the company is seen as a relationship of mutual interdependence in which the knowledge of the operational actors' about how to create construct causality contributes to the performance of the top management constituency. Also, the horizontal perspective of the organizational operation involves relationships of mutual interdependence.

Within the operative units, integration of the four dimensions is the condition for the activities to be performed and for succeeding in creating output. The integration is controlled by specialized, professional ways of reasoning. Effective coordination between operating units requires the output of one unit to be coherent with the demand of another unit. More specifically, effective performance management requires that the intentional objectives of the multiple constituencies be coherent from a number of perspectives: (i) vertically or hierarchically determined (i.e., through the power system reflecting the organizational values as represented by the top management); (ii) vertically, organizationally determined (i.e., the goal system of the activities must be constructed on the basis of the intentional values of the personnel); and (iii) horizontally, organizationally determined (i.e., the goal system in interdependent activities should be constructed so that they mutually support each other).

The goal and measurement system can be both quantitative and qualitative in nature. The quantitative measures at the various levels might not be of the same kind. Thus, at the top management level, the measures might mainly be of financial nature while at the operational level a limited number of nonfinancial measures might dominate. Both qualitatively and quantitatively concepts of the observational system need to be outlined by criteria and linked to a narrative integrating the four dimensions of reality. This implies that the goal and measurement system should be identifiable by their schemata of appearance and in relation to the possibilities and necessities that define its potentials and causal properties. In other words, the intentional objectives have to be linked to the multiple actors' operational method of creating successful action. In addition, the conceptual content must be linked to the sets of values that belong to individuals and groups of actors. Finally, the practical meaning of a concept must be communicated and understood by the actors in question.

As mentioned in Chapters 5 and 7, the formulation of a coherent goal system involves a management process of coauthorship and, hence, an actor-based approach. This requires that the goal formulation take place as a dialogue where actors at all the organizational levels participate as linking pins in the managers' effort of formulating and developing a coherent goal system. Through the dialogue, the manager uncovers their subordinates' subjective intentional values and situated knowledge and engages the individual to take responsibility for relevance of measures. The process takes place as an ongoing trust building and reflective interaction between the manager and the subordinates, where the manager seeks to influence the subordinates, gain insight into their intentions and operational methods, and use that insight to establish coherence between organizational units. Also, this process encourages and facilitates positive forces of learning through communicative interaction around factually possible actions and objectives within value range and, hence, cultivates organizational actors' operational methods on how to create construct causality.

In the following, we provide a sketch illustrating how actor-based learning approach that is informed by pragmatic constructivism works in performance measurement.

Use of Performance Measurement

In this section, we present an actor-based method of interaction used in the performance measurement for operational management at the service level. The method has been undertaken by an American supply chain manager who was assigned the challenging task of creating an effective supply chain system. This manager is employed in a Danish-owned subsidiary operating in the energy-manufacturing industry in the United States. First, we present the manager's way of communicating the intentional objective of the organizational unit and, subsequently, the manager's way of creating, validating, and developing knowledge and action on service-level performance through interaction with competent organizational actors (Trenca and Nørreklit 2017).

Communicating Intentionality

The objective of the supply chain unit is to meet the target of 85% *on-time delivery*, which is set for the unit by the organizational manager. Communicating the organizational intention, the supply chain manager integrates the measurement objective of on-time delivery with a narrative conceptualization of the implication of on-time delivery for organizational action and end results:

> So how do I know that *BU* is *satisfied*? If *I* have *components and stocks*, if I *have what they need*, and they can get it in a *timely manner*, and they can get their *things fixed, they're happy, I'm happy*. That's how I measure my job. And if so, I'm doing a good job—that's how I measure myself. And that is also how our *team* measures it. Thus, does *Laura* have *everything covered* for *Turkey* and *Australia*? As we have different *platforms*, I have to make sure that there is stock in *Denmark* to cover some of *Laura's regions*. And vice versa, as one of the platforms that *Laura* covers is affecting my stock over here.

In the quote, we see that there are multiple organizational units involved in the task of on-time delivery. The employees' perception of the objective of doing a good job is about making other units satisfied. The focus of the supply manager and their team should be on whether their units have the *components and stocks* and are *getting things fixed*, whether the other units *get what they need in a timely manner*, and whether their unit has *everything covered* from other organizational *platforms*. When everybody has what they need in a timely manner, the values of organizational actors are in a good state of affairs, the employees are *satisfied* and *happy*, and the organizational target is achieved. The intention of a functioning delivery practice is formulated in an affective conceptual language that links abstract measurement with a narrative expressing the practical meaning of the objective.

The Manager's Way of Creating Knowledge

The method of knowledge creation applied by the supply chain manager to construct a functioning collective practice is based on a string of observations and reflections on working with problems. Overall, they apply procedures for creating factual observational ground, managing motivational values, orchestrating proactive, true problem solving, and observing pragmatic truth and learning. In the following, we explain these knowledge procedures in more detail, leading to a conclusion on conceptualizing the manager's way of creating knowledge through interaction.

Creating Factual Observational Ground

Important for creating multiple understandings is the observation of factual performance and finding the *root cause* of the lack in performance:

> It's all about presenting the *facts*. . . . [We build trust] by knowing the *facts* and only presenting the *facts*. It's what it is, and I can have my opinions, and I can turn off my microphone, and I can say my opinions out loud to myself, but it's a delicate situation. [I ask:] *How come that you don't have my components for me?* You have to dig all the way down to what is the *root cause*.

The root cause of missing components is hindering construct causality, which is the reason it is crucial for the manager that they do something about it. Also, the quote indicates that questioning is pivotal when searching for the root cause. An elaboration of the manager's way of using questioning and observational facts in the search for root causes can be found in the following:

> . . . We have a target of 85, so if we got 99 we are doing very well. If we got a 60 or 40 [on-time delivery], then we *dig* in to see what

the issue was. *Was it* a transportation issue, was it that there was no stock? *Was it* too short the lead time from the customer? etc. . . . I'm *not blaming* transportation, I'm *not blaming* the service side. . . . The ultimate is not to place blame, but to *figure out what happens.* When you do the analysis you present the facts. And then [during the digging] someone may say "Ok, we only had 45% on time to require this week, this is the analysis that's been done." But it comes down to that SBU put down the same day for delivery, on their main component. . . . And I *dig* back in and do the analysis on that and I say "Ok, but I had a stock there when the order came in, so I'm not sure *why it didn't get* to Turkey on time." Some of it is simple as, they put an order today, and they say they want it delivered today. Then it's on the SBU side, because they didn't do their job correctly. Or I have it on the warehouse but the warehouse didn't ship it for two days. That's on the warehouse. But it's still on our group to figure out why it didn't happen. . . . Ok, so you have to start *digging* backwards. But, in the middle of that, one time you might go left, and one time you might go right. Depending on what the results are and your findings. . . . It's not knowledge, because I obviously do not know everything. It's *interpretation or understanding* what you're finding when you're doing that analysis that leads you to the next step. . . .

We witness that the observation of poor factual performance is the point of departure for a search process *digging* for root causes. There are many possibilities to consider when digging for a root cause, but it is the factual, possible one that has to be detected. The root cause is the missing action for creating construct causalities. In searching, the manager is asking for information on factual actions in the network of organizational actors: *Was it . . .? To figure out what happens, . . . and why it didn't get to . . .?* Through the manager's conversation process with the other actors, the factual actions are revealed, and whether these can be the cause of poor performance is reflected upon. The searching process follows a scheme of discovering the facts and developing diagnostic understanding. During the search process of questioning, the manager's knowledge is moving to an increasingly higher level of diagnosing the problems, and it goes on until the collected factual information provides a sufficient conceptual *interpretation* for *understanding* the phenomenon of poor factual performance. At this stage the root cause is found.

Overall, insight is shaped through knowing and discussing the factual course. Searching for facts, the supply chain manager is opening up the problem area until a sufficient level of understanding is reached about the problem and its causes. The actors are the source of information for finding the root cause. But the factual observations, and the plausible argumentation on how to relate them to the creation of problem, become the binding elements for the objectification of the problem.

Managing Motivational Values

In the quote presented earlier, the manager mentions that the search process is about *not blaming*. This is further emphasized in the following.

> . . . I do find that people on the supply chain side come to me and complain about the people at the service side (SBU). So I have to try to buffer that. And when I go to the SBU, I have to say: *"Ok, we've got an issue, and we need to know your opinion,"* instead of the tone of voice, or whatever I got from the supply chain side. I try to buffer and make it "We really need your help" instead of "We've got a problem" . . . You have to be the Nice Guy in the middle, so *I see it from the supply chain side* and *from the SBU side.* And when you do that, it creates confidence from the both sides. What you do is breaking [it] down to what is the issue, and then you say: "Ok but that really means this and this." . . . I'm trying to take the angry email and grasp, what is going on, and then you tone it down, and email somebody else and say: *"Ok, here's the issue, what can you do to help us?"* You want to make them feel like they are in control, whether it's going from the service side to the supply chain side or vice versa. *You want to make them feel like they are in control,* like they're helping with the outcome. . . .

The manager aims to transform factual claims loaded with negative emotions into factual claims calling for empathic insight: *"Ok, we've got an issue, and we need to know your opinion,"* instead of the tone of voice, or whatever I got from the *SBU*; and *"Ok, here's the issue, what can you do to help us?"* By being factual and not activating the angry emotions through blaming or communicating complaints, the manager takes away the separating force of the message. Instead, they create empathic attention to the problem, hence shaping the actor's participatory function. The explicit, formulated intention is to construct employees with a problem-solving ethos: *You want to make them feel like they are in control.*

The construction of the employees as problem solvers is important because the pivotal point of finding the root cause of a problem is solving it. Some problems are to be solved by making the employees internalize existing knowledge on what is the right action. Effective production of on-time delivery requires skilled and informed employees. The company has the job and process documentation on what is the right thing to do, which can be useful for new employees and service technicians.

Overall, in their interaction, the manager aims to positively influence the actors' mode of affect, which separates the manager from the other, so that the manager activates their participatory function. The manager aims to construct the employees as problem-solving actors rather than angry, self-centered bodies. Because the questioning and interpretation take place in interaction with the network of actors, the process also contributes to increasing the employees' knowledge and understanding of what is good and poor action.

Orchestrating Proactive, True Problem Solving

While some problems are about making the employees internalize existing knowledge on what is the right action, other problems will require the discovery of new knowledge. Discovering new solutions, the manager is digging for knowledge among the network of actors:

> Sometimes it's a matter of me *knowing who* to go to [and] *ask* who can resolve it. I don't claim to know the answers but I do know people [to whom] I can say *"I don't know what the answer is, this is what I am looking for, can you help me?"* I have to *ask the questions.* . . .
> I randomly start to send emails to people and say "Hey, I think

that you're *maybe the contact* for this. If you're not, who is it?" And I
get a name and then I *go to that person.* So that's how you dig to the
bottom, that's how you try to *establish those connections* and stuff.
It's just like *growing a tree and you know, just more,* more, more. So
a lot of people come to me and say "Hey I don't know the answer,
but I think I know who does. Let me contact them for you."

Thus, the manager's way of searching for solutions is governed by
questioning and interacting with other actors. Unlike in the foregoing
questioning, by detecting facts, the possible solutions are found in the
knowing and understanding of those with whom the manager is speaking.
The manager's strategy thus seems to rely on competent organizational
actors in establishing solutions. It is about finding the actors who know
something about solving the problem. In order for this manager to be
able to engage in such an investigation, they need to adopt an open and
humble attitude, which means that they have to be able to present their
inquiry openly and to nurture a state of psychological comfort with the
idea of not having the ready-to-use answers to the problem (Yanow 2009).

Sometimes, finding a solution requires the collaboration of multiple
actors. If so, the actors are brought together in a meeting to find solutions.

You have to bring the *stakeholders together* in a meeting, and we
have to initiate a whole new process or make an adaptation to a
current process. . . . You call them down and say *"Ok this is the
situation, we need to discuss,"* . . . And from that there might be
another meeting. You have to *make sure that you know whether
something is missing or whether the right people are not involved.* . . .
Maybe *somebody else knows something* that I don't and they get in
the meeting and they say "Oh yeah, we should be talking to (?),
or (?) should be involved in this." . . . And sometimes it is finance,
sometimes it is legal and I wouldn't even have thought of that. . . .
[When I can't figure things out] it is really good trying to *involve
everybody to* make sure that the process is complete.

We witness that the solution to the problem is not given by the manager
but by the employees. The manager asserts the problem situation and invites
other key actors into a process of coauthorship. Again, factual observations,

questioning, and reflection drive an interactive communication process. The collective reflective discovery process goes on until a possible solution is conceptualized by the collective of actors. During the discovery process, the manager's knowledge is moving to an increasingly higher level of diagnostic understanding of the possible solution to the problem. The binding element of the understanding seems to be the plausibility of the employees' argumentation on how to solve the problem. Thus, the validation of whether the solution is proactively true seems to be based on faith in the actors' knowledge and willingness to solve the problem.

Observing Pragmatic Truth and Learning

Orchestrating problem solving, the manager is giving the actors time to develop factual functioning solutions (construct causality):

> I figured out that this is the root cause, and this is what they're doing about it. Now we have to be patient, and *let that resolution take effect.*

The manager communicates to the actors that the problem-solving process may take time. However, the phrase *let that resolution take effect* indicates that at some point or the other a need will arise to check whether the resolution is based on pragmatic truth. Thus, eventually there will be an evaluation of whether the actor's idea for problem solving is pragmatically true. If the projected solution is not pragmatically true, it will display itself in lack of construct causality and, hence, initiate a new learning search into finding the root cause.

Sometimes, there is no immediate resolution. Then, as a final attempt in closing the gap between proactive truth and pragmatic truth, the manager used the technique of questioning a more experienced person, Soren, at a higher organizational level:

> Sometimes I present the facts to Soren and say "Ok, this is the issue. I've got my orders in, I've done what I was supposed to do and I'm not getting an end result." . . . then he will take the facts that are in the email, and say: "We have an issue here, what are we gonna do about it? Where is our order? Where is this material? When did the material come to the repair facility?" . . .

The quote reveals that the success of a local activity relies on the combination of different functions within the value chain. Accordingly, the validation of the proactive truth becomes challenging, because the effect of an action can rely on multiple interfering actors and can take time to materialize. Even though the process and methods are in place locally, and hence the proactive truth has been constructed rigorously, the proactive truth is impeded from becoming a pragmatic truth because failure occurs in other activities along the value chain. Nevertheless, taking the collective learning approach to the gap between the proactive truth and the pragmatic truth opens an avenue for digging across functional activities to detect the failure and hence to coauthor a solution for the problem together with managers at the higher organizational level. Thus, the manager's method of knowledge creation involves a reflective approach to developing the organizational method of controlling the specific operational practice.

Also, the manager is working with a learning theory of truth at the personal level:

> And sometimes your professional judgment is wrong and you hit a dead end. And then, I'm going back to take to the right because the left wasn't the right answer" . . . so a lot of that it's just learning from mistakes.

We witness an evaluation of whether the manager's professional judgment becomes pragmatically true. And if there is a truth gap, they make corrections. Mistakes are unavoidable and the challenge is how to learn. Accordingly, the manager's method of knowledge creation involves reflective learning at two levels. One relates to adjusting the operational method controlling the specific practice; the other relates to the personal knowledge system governing the creation of knowledge about controlling the specific practice.

But the manager is not born into an empathic and humble enquiring management approach. They have developed their knowledge procedure over time through a self-reflective learning process:

> Over the years I found that it's best to wait until you have all of the information that you need and then reply. . . .[Before], I wanted results right now. And then you find out that you get

better results when you put something out there nicely than when you are demanding.

We see that the development of their empathic and reflective management process involves the self-management of their personhood governing their knowledge creation process.

Some Conclusions on the Manager's Creation of Knowledge

The procurement manager tries to construct a successful way of working that involves a group of relevant staff so that the aim of on-time delivery is achieved. Their approach to this is, therefore, people centered and is based on querying, reviewing, and gaining knowledge about the problem situation, discussing with others for agreeing on problems, and considerable contemplation of how things work in the firm. Thus, contact with others to conduct these activities contributes to the identification of the causes of poor results. This type of group collaboration generates ideas from all staff and aids them all in developing a factual understanding of the difficulties faced. In doing this, the manager enhances their skills in problem diagnosis and the pragmatic approach in how to address the situation. The duration of these activities is dependent on factual information being gathered to produce insights about the root causes of poor results and then tailoring solutions for them.

The manager has realized that comprehending their situation depends on their interpreting and integrating the ideas from a range of specialist perspectives. Their capability to develop a functioning enquiry group facilitates analytical decision making and planning in their firm. They do not simply impose the views they hold on problem causes and solutions but use other managers' views to identify the root causes and factual possible solutions. Their ability to pose pertinent questions teases out relevant knowledge and this helps to bind the group into ownership of the beliefs they rely on and the actions that they take. Their interventions also ensure that firm values are enshrined in planning and decision making. The group is intrinsically cooperative and constructive rather than antagonistic and critical, and this enhances their productivity.

It is noticeable that the manager's querying is directed to ascertain whether there are any shortcomings in currently held beliefs about the construct causality. They do this in a manner that is not confrontational and so helps to construct group acceptance of new beliefs that will achieve on-time delivery.

The managerial group are given freedom to generate solutions that meet firm's values. The capabilities of all the managers are mutually recognized and used to build a shared proactive truth derived from their judgments. When actual results become known and a truth gap is apparent the manager will initiate investigation to determine how it has come about. Revision of causality connections will take place based on new facts that emerge through group consideration of the situation.

The manager's communication style fosters goodwill and trust within the group. This creates the condition where information is freely shared, analysis is cooperative, and, thus, problem diagnosis and action is consensual. However, the goal of removing barriers to on-time delivery remains paramount as the manager ensures its prominence is retained in group discussions.

In these ways, the manager draws on the four dimensions of reality to attain the firm's practical aims. They ensure that the group's conceptions of proactive truth have to be assessed in the light of pragmatic truth and that it is this which generates a learning process that steadily improves managerial action over time.

Discussion Questions

1. Drawing on pragmatic constructivism, discuss the strength and weaknesses of a digital-based performance measurement system such as TripAdvisor? How do the user measures relate to the four dimensions of pragmatic constructivism (facts, possibilities, values, and communication)? What are the blind spots of integration embedded in the system? What might be the consequences of digital-based performance measurement?

2. Drawing on pragmatic constructivism, you are asked to design a system for the performance management of a marketing and sales unit of an organization. What measures will you suggest? How will you use those measures?

CHAPTER 9

Conclusion

Falconer Mitchell and Hanne Nørreklit

Understanding how managers take successful actions is a prerequisite for explaining and providing guidance on how successful management performance can be achieved. This text has shown how a particular philosophy of human action taking can fulfill this basic role. It has demonstrated that the managerial processes underlying successful practice can be identified and used to provide the guidance that can lead to successful management that can also be improved over time. Managerial action is founded on the four key dimensions of the reality of the "world" in which the manager operates: facts, action possibilities, values to be attained, and communication. The success of managerial action is dependent on these dimensions both corresponding to the reality of the situation and whether they are integrated coherently with each other. Identification of relevant facts and the action possibilities deriving from them provides the situational reality of the manager. Action possibilities thus selected will then have to fit not only with the identified facts but also meet recognized managerial and organizational values and intentions. To achieve this, they have to be derived from and disseminated through strong communication systems that build, test, and reflect on managerial beliefs about how "things" work in their organization.

This philosophical approach requires managers to be both people centered and reflective in their work. Without people, organizations do not function, and managers will therefore have to hold sound beliefs about how employees will react to their actions. These beliefs are developed as part of a learning experience as managers act and reflect on the impacts of their actions in ways that will strengthen their organizational beliefs.

Reflection is also necessary upon the following: (i) selection of facts deemed relevant to issues under consideration by management, (ii) identification of action possibilities created by identified facts, (iii) ascertaining the values achievement inherent in possible actions, and (iv) undertaking the communications needed to design and initiate action. Through such reflection, managerial beliefs can become more accurate, and, consequently, managerial action becomes more successful over time.

References

Anthony, R.N., and V. Govindarajan. 2007. *Management Control Systems.* Vol. 12. New York, NY: McGraw-Hill.

Arbnor, I., and B. Bjerke. 2008. *Methodology for Creating Business Knowledge.* Thousand Oaks, CA: Sage.

Asch, D. 1992. "Strategic Control: A Problem Looking for a Solution." *Long Range Planning* 25, no. 2, pp. 105–10

Bhimani, A., C.T. Horngren, S.M. Datar, and G. Foster. 2008. *Management and Cost Accounting.* Vol. 1. Essex: Pearson Education.

Cetina, K.K. 2001. "Objectual Practice." In *The Practice Turn in Contemporary Theory*, eds. T.R. Schatzki, K.K. Cetina and E. von Savigny, 175–88. London: Routledge.

Chambers, R.J. 1966. *Accounting Evaluation and Economic Behaviour.* Upper Saddle River, NJ: Prentice-Hall.

Chandler, A.D., Jr. 1962/1998. *Strategy and Structure: Chapters in the History of the American Industrial Enterprise.* Cambridge, MA: MIT Press.

Cinquini, L., F. Mitchell, H. Nørreklit, and A. Tenucci. 2012. "Methodologies of Performance Measurement." In *Routledge Companion to Cost Management*, eds. F. Mitchell, H. Nørreklit, and M. Jakobsen. New York and London: Routledge.

Ghoshal, S. 2005. "Bad Management Theories Are Destroying Good Management Practices." *Academy of Management Learning & Education* 4, no. 1, pp. 75–91.

Heijltjes, M. 1995. *Organizational Fit or Failure.* Maastricht: University of Maastricht Press.

Jakobsen, M., I.-L. Johanson, and H. Nørreklit. eds. 2011. *An Actor's Approach to Management: Conceptual Framework and Company Practices.* Copenhagen: DJOEF.

Jakobsen, M., F. Mitchell, H. Nørreklit, and M. Trenca. 2019. "Educating Management Accountants as Business Partners: Pragmatic Constructivism as an Alternative Pedagogical Paradigm for Teaching

Management Accounting at Master's Level." *Qualitative Research in Accounting and Management* 16, no. 2.

Jensen, M.C., and W.H. Meckling. 1976. "Theory of the Firm: Managerial Behavior, Agency Cost and Ownership Structure." *Journal of Financial Economics* 3, no. 4, pp. 305–60.

Kaplan, R.S., and A.A. Atkinson. 2015. *Advanced Management Accounting.* New Delhi, India: PHI Learning.

Kaplan, R.S., and D.P. Norton. 1996. *The Balanced Scorecard—Translating Strategy into Action.* Boston, MA: Harvard Business School Press.

Laine, T., T. Korhonen, P. Suomala, and A. Rantamaa. 2016. "Boundary Subjects and Boundary Objects in Accounting Fact Construction and Communication". *Qualitative Research in Accounting & Management* 13, no. 3, pp. 303–29.

March, J.G. 1987. "Ambiguity and Accounting: The Elusive Link between Information and Decision Making." *Accounting, Organizations and Society* 12, no. 2, pp. 153–68.

Miles, R.E., and C.C. Snow. 1978. *Organizational Strategy, Structure and Process.* New York, NY: McGraw-Hill,

Merchant, K.A. 1985. *Control in Business Organizations.* Boston, MA: Harvard Graduate School of Business.

Merchant, K., and W.A. Van der Stede. 2012. *Performance Measurement, Evaluation and Incentives.* Essex: Pearson Education.

Mitchell, F., L. Nielsen, H. Nørreklit, and L. Nørreklit. 2013. "Scoring Strategic Performance—A Pragmatic Constructivist Approach to Strategic Performance Measurement." *Journal of Management and Governance* 17, no. 1, pp. 5–34.

Neely, A.D. ed. 2007. *Business Performance Measurement.* Cambridge, MA: Cambridge University Press.

Neely, A.D., and C. Adams. 2001. "The Performance Prism Perspective." *Journal of Cost Management* 15, no. 1, pp. 7–15.

Nielsen, L.B., F. Mitchell, and H. Nørreklit. 2015. "Management Accounting and Decision Making: Two Case Studies of Outsourcing." *Accounting Forum* 19, no. 1, pp. 64–82.

Nørreklit, H. 2000. "The Balance on the Balanced Scorecard—A Critical Analysis of Some of Its Assumptions." *Management Accounting Research* 11, no. 1, pp. 65–88.

Nørreklit, H., ed. 2017. *A Philosophy of Management Accounting: A Pragmatic Constructivist Approach.* New York and London: Routledge.

Nørreklit, H., F. Mitchell, and L.B. Nielsen. 2017. "Reflective Planning and Decision-Making." In *A Philosophy of Management Accounting: A Pragmatic Constructivist Approach*, ed. H. Nørreklit. New York and London: Routledge.

Nørreklit, H., L. Nørreklit, and P. Israelsen. 2006. "Validity of Management Control Topoi? Towards Constructivist Pragmatism." *Management Accounting Research* 17, no. 1, pp. 42–71.

Nørreklit, H., L. Nørreklit, and F. Mitchell. 2016. "Understanding Practice Generalisation—Opening the Research/Practice Gap." *Qualitative Research in Accounting and Management* 13, no. 3, pp. 278–302.

Nørreklit, H., L. Nørreklit, and F. Mitchell. 2007. "Theoretical Conditions for Validity in Accounting Performance Measurement." In *Business Performance Measurement*, ed. A. Neely. Cambridge, MA: Cambridge University Press.

Nørreklit, H., L. Nørreklit, and F. Mitchell. 2010. "Towards a Paradigmatic Foundations of Accounting Practice. *Accounting, Auditing and Accountability Journal* 23, no. 6, pp. 733–58.

Nørreklit, H., L. Nørreklit, and F. Mitchell. 2013. "Thinking: What Can Accountants Gain from Applying the Principles of Pragmatic Constructivism?" *Financial Management*. 10, October

Nørreklit, L. 2017. "Actor Reality Construction." In *A Philosophy of Management Accounting: A Pragmatic Constructivist Approach*, ed. H. Nørreklit. New York and London: Routledge.

Nørreklit, L. 2011. "Actors and Reality: A Conceptual Framework for Creative Governance." In *An Actor's Approach to Management: Conceptual Framework and Company Practices*, eds. M. Jakobsen, I.-L. Johanson, and H. Nørreklit, 7–37. Copenhagen: DJOEF.

Puxty, A.G. 1985. *Critiques of Agency Theory in Accountancy*, Issues in Accountability XII, The University of Sheffield.

Rappaport, A. 1997. *Creating Shareholder Value: A Guide for Managers and Investors.* New York, NY: The Free Press.

Simons, R. 1995. *Levers of Control.* Boston, MA: Harvard Business School Press.

Solomon, D. 1965. *Divisional Performance: Measurement and Control.* Illinois: Irwin.

Sterling, R.R. 1979. *Theory of the Measurement of Enterprise Income.* Lawrence: The University Press of Kansas.

Trenca, M., and H. Nørreklit. 2017. "Actor-Based Performance Management." In *A Philosophy of Management Accounting: A Pragmatic Constructivist Approach*, ed. H. Nørreklit. New York and London: Routledge.

Vaivio, J. (2008). "Qualitative Management Accounting Research: Rationale, Pitfalls and Potential." *Qualitative Research in Accounting & Management* 5, no. 1, pp. 64–86.

von Wright, G.H. 1983. *Practical Reason.* Oxford: Basil Blackwell.

Yanow, D. 2009. "Ways of Knowing: Passionate Humility and Reflective Practice in Research and Management." *The American Review of Public Administration* 39, no. 6, pp. 579–601.

List of Contributors

Lars Braad Nielsen, PhD, is manager at the global consultancy company Quartz (Oslo, Norway). He has done research on outsourcing decision making and principal–agent theory. He has experience carrying out cost optimization and restructuring of projects in leading international companies.

Lennart Nørreklit, Drfil, has been professor of philosophy and management at Aalborg University, Denmark. His research interests include the concept of reality, cross-cultural philosophy, methodology of social science, and philosophy of the "good life." He has developed the philosophical basis of pragmatic constructivism.

Mihaela Trenca, PhD, is financial manager at the cultural NGO organization, Albagnano Healing Meditation Centre, and an affiliated assistant professor at Scuola Superiore Sant' Anna, Italy. Her research interests lie in the area of performance management, with a particular focus on performance management practices allowing the development of actors' awareness of the multiple interdependencies that shape organizational reality.

About the Authors

Falconer Mitchell, BCom, CA, is professor of management accounting at the University of Edinburgh. He has been the chairman of CIMA's research board. His research interests lie in the area of managerial accounting with particular reference to cost management and management accounting change processes. He is also heavily involved in developing pragmatic constructivism within the accounting field.

Hanne Nørreklit, PhD, is professor of management accounting and control, at School of Business and Social Science, Aarhus University, Denmark. Her research areas include performance management and control, management rhetoric, and validity issues in accounting and management. She is the coordinator of the research network on pragmatic constructivism (see http://mgmt.au.dk/research/organisation-strategy-and-accounting/osa-research/networks/actor-reality-construction/).

Index

OTHER TITLES IN THE MANAGERIAL ACCOUNTING COLLECTION

Kenneth A. Merchant, University of Southern California, *Editor*

- *Revenue Management: A Path to Increased Profits, Second Edition* by Ronald J. Huefner
- *Cents of Mission: Using Cost Management and Control to Accomplish Your Goal* by Dale R. Geiger
- *Sustainability Reporting: Getting Started, Second Edition* by Gwendolen B. White
- *Lies, Damned Lies, and Cost Accounting: How Capacity Management Enables Improved Cost and Cash Flow Management* by Reginald Tomas Lee, Sr.
- *Strategic Management Accounting: Delivering Value in a Changing Business Environment Through Integrated Reporting* by Sean Stein Smith
- *Strategic Managerial Accounting—A Primer for the IT Professional* by Gopal Saxena
- *Strategic Cost Analysis, Second Edition* by Roger Hussey and Audra Ong
- *Management Accounting in Support of Strategy: How Management Accounting Can Aid the Strategic Management Process* by Graham S. Pitcher
- *Strategic Cost Transformation: Using Business Domain Management to Improve Cost Data, Analysis, and Management* by Reginald Tomas Lee
- *From Value Pricing to Pricing Value: Using Science, Psychology, and Systems to Attract Higher Paying Clients to Your Accounting Firm* by Rhondalynn Korolak

Announcing the Business Expert Press Digital Library

Concise e-books business students need for classroom and research

This book can also be purchased in an e-book collection by your library as

- *a one-time purchase,*
- *that is owned forever,*
- *allows for simultaneous readers,*
- *has no restrictions on printing, and*
- *can be downloaded as PDFs from within the library community.*

Our digital library collections are a great solution to beat the rising cost of textbooks. E-books can be loaded into their course management systems or onto students' e-book readers. The **Business Expert Press** digital libraries are very affordable, with no obligation to buy in future years. For more information, please visit **www.businessexpertpress.com/librarians**. To set up a trial in the United States, please email **sales@businessexpertpress.com**.